Using this atlas

D0491848

How to use this atlas

The atlas is in five colour coded sections. These are shown on the **List of contents** on the page opposite.

There are two ways to find information in this atlas.

- Firstly, if you are looking for a particular topic, look for it on the **List of contents** on the page opposite or on the **Subject list** on this page. For example, maps showing Energy resources can be found on pages 15 and 41.

- Secondly, if you are looking for a particular place or feature, look for the name of the place in the **Index of place names** on pages 64–65. You can refer to page 63 **Finding places** to help you find the place on the map. If you know roughly where a particular name occurs, you can use the **Key map of the continents** below or the **List of contents** to find the map page number and then look for it on the map.

Subject list

ARCTIC
page 62

ARCTIC OCEAN

UK AND IRELAND
pages 24–27

EUROPE
pages 50–51

ASIA
pages 52–53

NORTH AMERICA
pages 58–59

PACIFIC OCEAN

AFRICA
pages 54–55

INDIAN OCEAN

SOUTH AMERICA
pages 60–61

PACIFIC OCEAN

ATLANTIC OCEAN

AUSTRALIA AND OCEANIA
pages 56–57

ANTARCTICA
page 62

SOUTHERN OCEAN

Key map of the continents

COPYRIGHT PHILIP'S

What is a map?

These small maps explain the meaning of some of the lines and colours on the atlas maps.

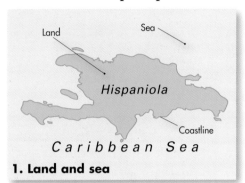

1. Land and sea

This is how an island is shown on a map. The land is coloured green and the sea is blue. The coastline is a blue line.

2. Rivers and lakes

There are some lakes on the island and rivers that flow down to the sea.

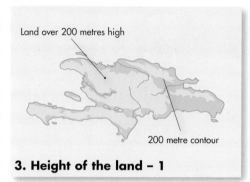

3. Height of the land – 1

This map shows the land over 200 metres high in a lighter colour. The height of the land is shown by contour lines and layer colours.

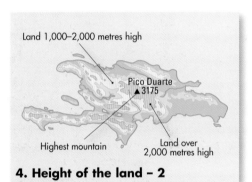

4. Height of the land – 2

This map shows more contour lines and layer colours. It shows that the highest mountain is in the centre of the island and that it is over 3,000 metres high.

5. Countries

This is a way of showing different information about the island. It shows that the island is divided into two countries. They are separated by a country boundary.

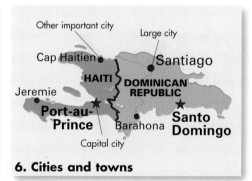

6. Cities and towns

There are cities and towns on the island. The two capital cities are shown with a special symbol. Other large or important cities are shown by a red circle.

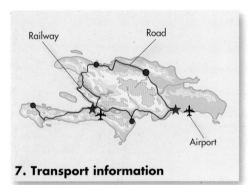

7. Transport information

This map shows the most important roads, railways and airports. Transport routes connect the cities and towns.

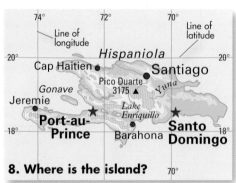

8. Where is the island?

This map gives lines of latitude and longitude and shows where the island is in the world. Page 59 in the atlas shows the same island on a map at a different scale.

9. A complete map

This map is using the country colouring and showing the letter-figure codes used in the index.

2

Map information

Symbols

Page 17

A map symbol shows the position of something – for example, circles for towns or an aeroplane for an airport.

Page 46

On some maps a dot or a symbol stands for a large number – for example, 500,000 people or cities with over 10 million people.

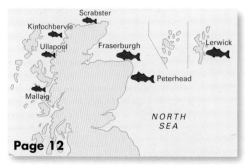

Page 12

The size of the symbol can be bigger or smaller, to show different numbers. The symbol here shows fishing ports in the UK.

Colours

Page 51

Colours are used on some maps so that separate areas, such as countries, as in this map, can be seen clearly.

Page 36

Patterns on maps often spread across country borders. This map shows different types of vegetation in the world.

Page 8

On other maps, areas that are the same in some way have the same colour to show patterns. This map shows rainfall.

Page 40

Colours that are lighter or darker are used on some maps to show less or more of something. This map shows farming.

Graphs and charts

Graphs and charts are used to give more information about subjects shown on the maps. A graph shows how something changes over time.

This graph shows the rainfall for each month in a year as a blue bar that can be measured on the scale at the side of the graph.

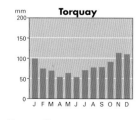

Page 8

This diagram is called a pie-chart. It shows how you can divide a total into its parts. It shows where the food eaten in the UK comes from.

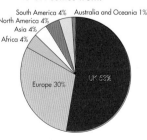

Page 12

This is a bar-chart. It is another way of showing a total divided into parts.

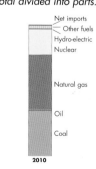

Page 15

Scale

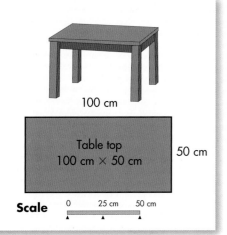

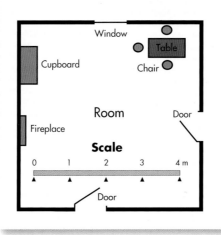

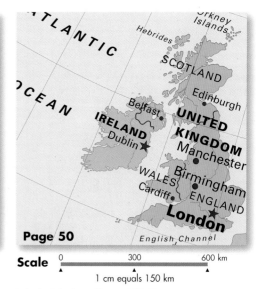

This is a drawing of the top of a table, looking down on it. It is 100 cm long and 50 cm wide. The drawing measures 4 × 2 cm. It is drawn to scale: 1 cm on the drawing equals 25 cm on the table.

This is a plan of a room looking down from above. 1 cm on the plan equals 1 metre in the room. The same table is shown, but now at a smaller scale. Use the scale bar to find the measurements of other parts of the room.

This is a map of an area in the city of Bath. Large buildings can be seen but other buildings are too small to show. Below are atlas maps of different scales.

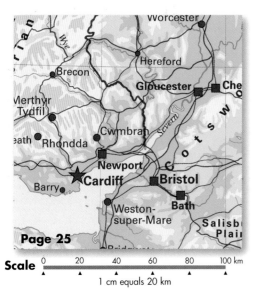

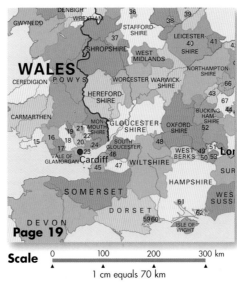

Scale bars

This distance represents 1 mile

This distance represents 1 kilometre

These examples of scale bars are at the scale of 1 cm equals 0.5 km

Signposts still have miles on them. 1 mile = 1.6 km, or 10 miles is the same as 16 kilometres.
On the maps of the UK and Ireland and the continents kilometre scale bars are used. On the maps of the continents, where you cannot see the UK and Ireland, a small map is shown to give you some idea of size and scale.

UK & IRELAND
On same scale

Direction

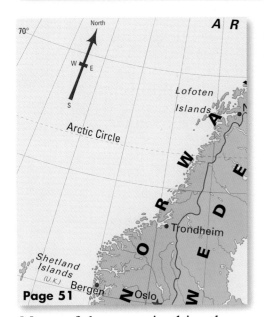

Page 51

The Cardinal Points

North
(N) 0°

West
(W) 270°

East
(E) 90°

South
(S) 180°

The Eight-Point Compass

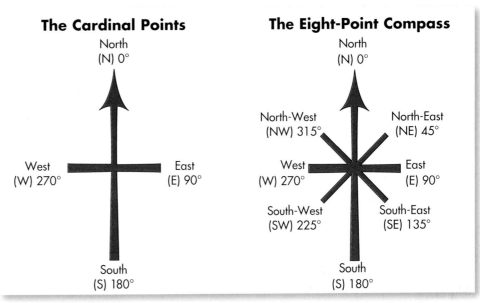

North
(N) 0°

North-West
(NW) 315°

North-East
(NE) 45°

West
(W) 270°

East
(E) 90°

South-West
(SW) 225°

South-East
(SE) 135°

South
(S) 180°

Many of the maps in this atlas have a North Point showing the direction of north. It points in the same direction as the lines of longitude. The four main directions shown are called the cardinal points.

Direction is measured in degrees. This diagram shows the degree numbers for each cardinal point. The direction is measured clockwise from north. The diagram on the right shows all the points of the compass and the divisions between the cardinal points. For example, between north and east there is north-east, between south and west is south-west. You can work out the cardinal points at your home by looking for the sun rising in the east and setting in the west.

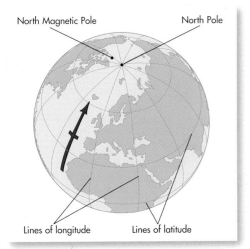

Lines of longitude   Lines of latitude

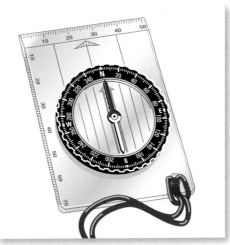

Page 25

The Earth has a spot near the North Pole that is called the Magnetic Pole. If a piece of metal that was magnetized at one end was left to float, then the magnetized tip would point to the North Magnetic Pole.

The needle of a compass is magnetized and it always points north. If you know where you are and want to go to another place, you can measure your direction from a map and use a compass to guide you.

North is at the top of this map. Look at the points of the compass on the diagram above and the positions of places on the map. Taunton is north-east of Exeter and Dorchester is south-east of Taunton.

Rocks, mountains and rivers

Rocks

This map shows the different types of rock in Great Britain and Ireland.

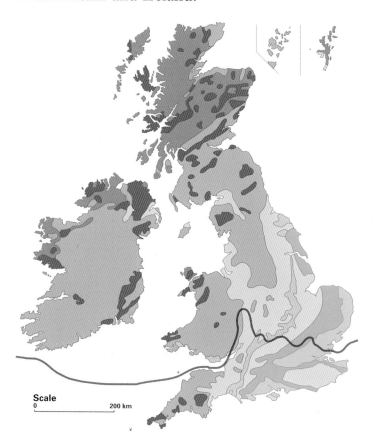

Scale
0   200 km

Longest rivers
(length in kilometres)

1. Shannon 370
2. Severn 354
3. Thames 335
4. Trent.............................. 297
5. Aire............................... 259
6. Great Ouse...................... 230
7. Wye 215
8. Tay................................ 188
9. Nene 161
10. Clyde............................. 158

The longest river in Northern Ireland is the River Bann (129 kilometres). The longest river completely in Wales is the Tywi (109 kilometres).

Largest lakes
(area in square kilometres)

1. Lough Neagh 382
2. Lough Corrib..................... 168
3. Lough Derg 120
4. Lower Lough Erne 105
5. Loch Lomond 71
6. Loch Ness 57

The largest lake in England is Windermere (15 square kilometres). The largest lake in Wales is Llyn Vyrnwy (8 square kilometres).

Largest islands
(area in square kilometres)

1. Great Britain.................229,880
2. Ireland 84,400
3. Lewis and Harris...............2,225
4. Skye..............................1,666
5. Shetland (Mainland)............967
6. Mull................................899
7. Anglesey 714
8. Islay...............................615
9. Isle of Man 572
10. Isle of Wight....................381

Highest mountains
(height in metres)

In Scotland:
  Ben Nevis..........................1,344
In Wales:
  Snowdon..........................1,085
In Ireland:
  Carrauntoohill 1,041
In England:
  Scafell Pike..........................978
In Northern Ireland:
  Slieve Donard......................852

Type of rock

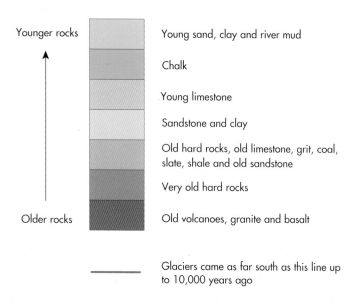

Younger rocks → / ← Older rocks

- Young sand, clay and river mud
- Chalk
- Young limestone
- Sandstone and clay
- Old hard rocks, old limestone, grit, coal, slate, shale and old sandstone
- Very old hard rocks
- Old volcanoes, granite and basalt

——— Glaciers came as far south as this line up to 10,000 years ago

Lewis and Harris — Skye — Mull — Islay — Loch Ness — Ben Nevis — Loch Lomond — Tay — Clyde — Shetland (Mainland) — **Great Britain** — Lough Neagh — Lower Lough Erne — Slieve Donard — Scafell Pike — Windermere — Lough Corrib — **Ireland** — Anglesey — Isle of Man — Lough Derg — Snowdon — Llyn Vyrnwy — Aire — Trent — Nene — Severn — Great Ouse — Shannon — Carrauntoohill — Wye — Thames — Isle of Wight

Scale
0   200 km

Height of the land in the UK and Ireland

metres
Over 500
100–500
0–100
sea level
below sea level
Sea and lakes

Shetland Islands

Fair Isle

Orkney Islands

Cape Wrath

Pentland Firth

Duncansby Head

North

W · E

S

Outer Hebrides

Lewis

Harris

St. Kilda

Inner Hebrides

Skye

North West Highlands

Moray Firth

Kinnairds Head

Spey

Loch Ness

Cairn Gorm 1245

Grampian Mountains

ATLANTIC

OCEAN

Mull

Ben Nevis 1344

Tay

NORTH

SEA

Islay

Loch Lomond

Firth of Forth

Arran

Clyde

Firth of Clyde

North Channel

Southern Uplands

Tweed

Great Britain

Malin Head

Ireland

Donegal Bay

Bann

Lower Lough Erne

Lough Neagh

Mourne Mountains

852
Slieve Donard

Tyne

Solway Firth

Lake District

Scafell Pike ▲ 978

Pennines

Tees

Isle of Man

Windermere

Flamborough Head

Lough Corrib

Lough Ree

Boyne

IRISH SEA

Liverpool Bay

Aire

Ouse

Humber

Galway Bay

Shannon

Lough Derg

Liffey

Wicklow Mountains

Anglesey

Snowdon ▲ 1085

Mersey

Trent

The Wash

Barrow

Cardigan Bay

Llyn Vyrnwy

Dee

The Fens

Nene

Great Ouse

Carrauntoohill 1041

Blackwater

Suir

Cambrian Mountains

Severn

Avon

Cotswolds

Chiltern Hills

Cape Clear

St. George's Channel

Tywi

Wye

Thames

North Downs

Bristol Channel

Exmoor

Salisbury Plain

South Downs

Strait of Dover

France

CELTIC SEA

Dartmoor

Lyme Bay

Isle of Wight

Beachy Head

English Channel

Scale
0   100 km   200 km

Land's End

Isles of Scilly

France

Channel Islands

COPYRIGHT PHILIP'S

7

Weather and climate

Rainfall is measured at many places every day. Each year, all the measurements are put together and graphs are made, like the ones shown on this page. Experts in the weather use these measurements to find out the average amount of rainfall for each place and for each year. They can then show this on climate maps, like the map below. Graphs and maps are also made for average temperatures and other types of weather (see opposite page). These help the experts to see patterns in the weather over a long period of time. These patterns in the weather show a country's climate. The maps on these pages show you the climate of the UK and Ireland.

If you collect the rainfall each day and measure it, then you could draw a graph like this.

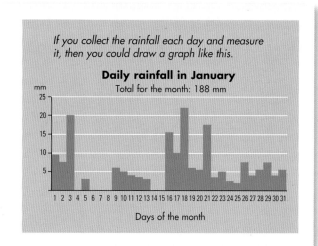

Daily rainfall in January
Total for the month: 188 mm

Days of the month

Rainfall

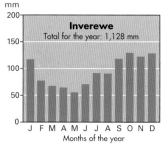

Inverewe
Total for the year: 1,128 mm
Months of the year

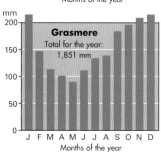

Grasmere
Total for the year: 1,851 mm
Months of the year

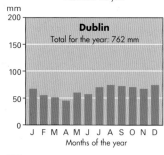

Dublin
Total for the year: 762 mm
Months of the year

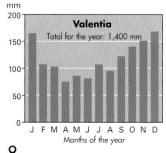

Valentia
Total for the year: 1,400 mm
Months of the year

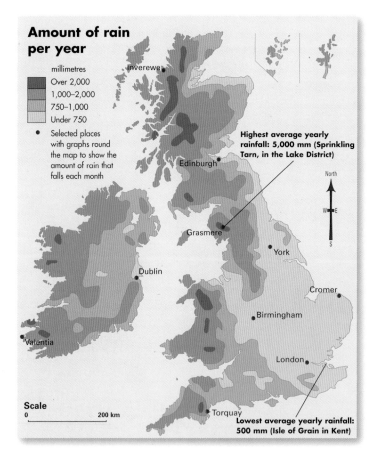

Amount of rain per year

millimetres
- Over 2,000
- 1,000–2,000
- 750–1,000
- Under 750

● Selected places with graphs round the map to show the amount of rain that falls each month

Highest average yearly rainfall: 5,000 mm (Sprinkling Tarn, in the Lake District)

North
W–E
S

Lowest average yearly rainfall: 500 mm (Isle of Grain in Kent)

Scale
0   200 km

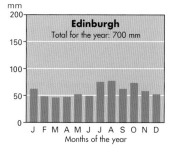

Edinburgh
Total for the year: 700 mm
Months of the year

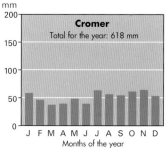

York
Total for the year: 639 mm
Months of the year

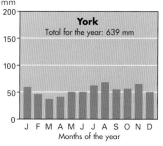

Cromer
Total for the year: 618 mm
Months of the year

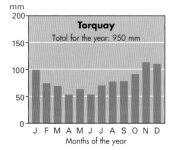

Torquay
Total for the year: 950 mm
Months of the year

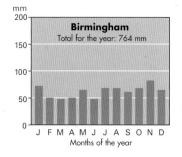

Birmingham
Total for the year: 764 mm
Months of the year

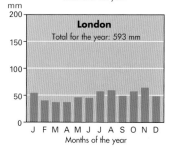

London
Total for the year: 593 mm
Months of the year

Wind

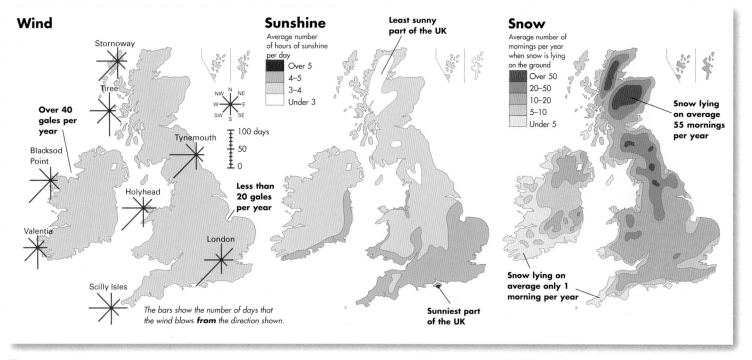

Stornoway

Tiree

Over 40 gales per year

Blacksod Point

Tynemouth

Holyhead

Valentia

London

Scilly Isles

Less than 20 gales per year

*The bars show the number of days that the wind blows **from** the direction shown.*

NW N NE
W E
SW S SE

100 days
50
0

Sunshine

Average number of hours of sunshine per day

Over 5
4–5
3–4
Under 3

Least sunny part of the UK

Sunniest part of the UK

Snow

Average number of mornings per year when snow is lying on the ground

Over 50
20–50
10–20
5–10
Under 5

Snow lying on average 55 mornings per year

Snow lying on average only 1 morning per year

Temperature

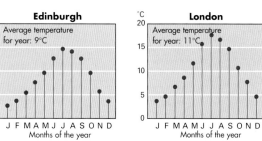

Birmingham
°C
20
15
10
5
0
Average temperature for year: 10°C
J F M A M J J A S O N D
Months of the year

Dublin
°C
20
15
10
5
0
Average temperature for year: 10°C
J F M A M J J A S O N D
Months of the year

Edinburgh
°C
20
15
10
5
0
Average temperature for year: 9°C
J F M A M J J A S O N D
Months of the year

London
°C
20
15
10
5
0
Average temperature for year: 11°C
J F M A M J J A S O N D
Months of the year

Plymouth
°C
20
15
10
5
0
Average temperature for year: 11°C
J F M A M J J A S O N D
Months of the year

Winter temperature

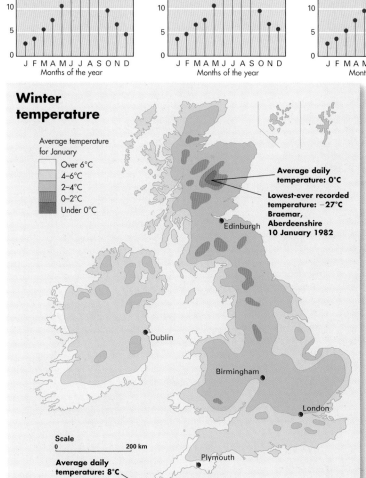

Average temperature for January

Over 6°C
4–6°C
2–4°C
0–2°C
Under 0°C

Average daily temperature: 0°C

Lowest-ever recorded temperature: –27°C Braemar, Aberdeenshire 10 January 1982

Edinburgh

Dublin

Birmingham

London

Scale
0   200 km

Plymouth

Average daily temperature: 8°C

Summer temperature

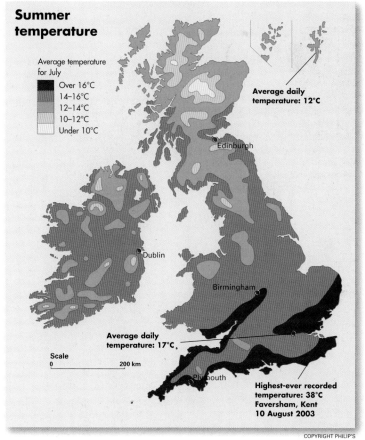

Average temperature for July

Over 16°C
14–16°C
12–14°C
10–12°C
Under 10°C

Average daily temperature: 12°C

Edinburgh

Dublin

Birmingham

Average daily temperature: 17°C

Plymouth

Scale
0   200 km

Highest-ever recorded temperature: 38°C Faversham, Kent 10 August 2003

Water

Rainfall areas in the UK and Ireland

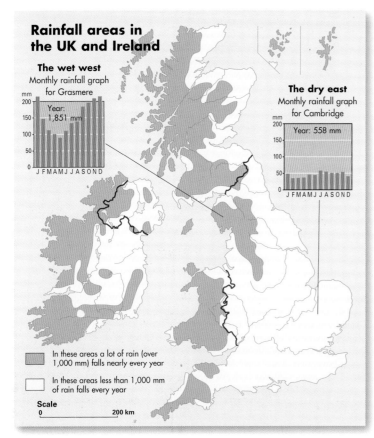

The wet west
Monthly rainfall graph for Grasmere

Year: 1,851 mm

The dry east
Monthly rainfall graph for Cambridge

Year: 558 mm

In these areas a lot of rain (over 1,000 mm) falls nearly every year

In these areas less than 1,000 mm of rain falls every year

Scale
0 — 200 km

Reservoirs and boreholes

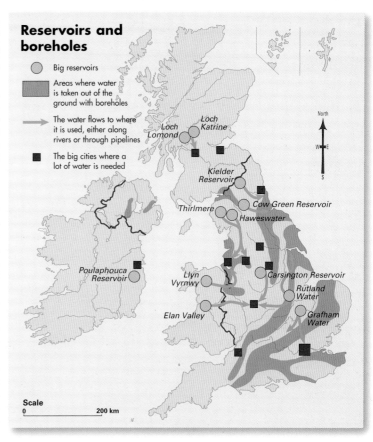

Big reservoirs

Areas where water is taken out of the ground with boreholes

The water flows to where it is used, either along rivers or through pipelines

The big cities where a lot of water is needed

Loch Lomond
Loch Katrine
Kielder Reservoir
Thirlmere
Cow Green Reservoir
Haweswater
Poulaphouca Reservoir
Llyn Vyrnwy
Carsington Reservoir
Rutland Water
Elan Valley
Grafham Water

North

Scale
0 — 200 km

Sources of river pollution

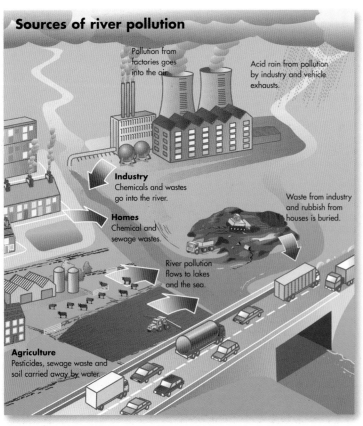

Pollution from factories goes into the air.

Acid rain from pollution by industry and vehicle exhausts.

Industry
Chemicals and wastes go into the river.

Homes
Chemical and sewage wastes.

Waste from industry and rubbish from houses is buried.

River pollution flows to lakes and the sea.

Agriculture
Pesticides, sewage waste and soil carried away by water.

Pollution

Percentage of rivers of very good quality

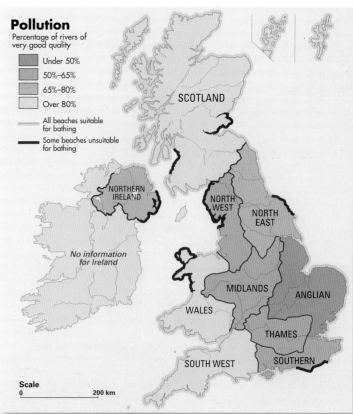

Under 50%

50%–65%

65%–80%

Over 80%

All beaches suitable for bathing

Some beaches unsuitable for bathing

SCOTLAND

NORTHERN IRELAND

No information for Ireland

NORTH WEST

NORTH EAST

MIDLANDS

ANGLIAN

WALES

THAMES

SOUTH WEST

SOUTHERN

Scale
0 — 200 km

Up to 17,400 million litres of water are used each day in the UK. Over half the water is used by people in their homes. About a third is used to make electricity. The rest is used in farms, fish farms and factories. In the UK each person uses about 150 litres of water per day. On the right are some of the ways that water is used in the home.

To make one car can use up to 40,000 litres of water. To brew one pint of beer needs 8 pints of water.

How we use water in the home

Showering and bathing	33%
Flushing the toilet	30%
Clothes washing	13%
Washing up	8%
Outdoors	7%
Drinking	4%

Flooding

Around 5 million people, in 2 million properties, live in flood risk areas in England and Wales. In summer 2007 there were several periods of extreme rainfall which led to widespread flooding.

The Environment Agency has an important role in warning people about the risk of flooding, and in reducing the likelihood of flooding from rivers and the sea.

Flood risk in England and Wales

Areas at greatest risk from flooding

Counties worst affected by flooding in summer 2007

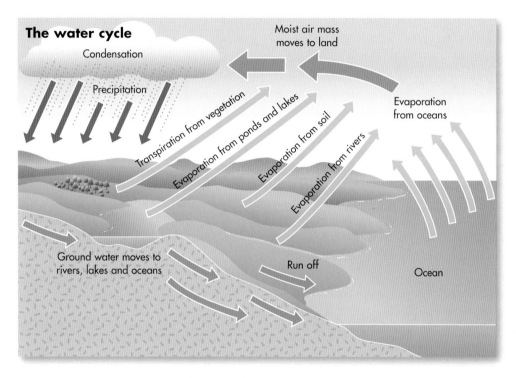

The water cycle

Condensation
Precipitation
Moist air mass moves to land
Transpiration from vegetation
Evaporation from ponds and lakes
Evaporation from soil
Evaporation from rivers
Evaporation from oceans
Ground water moves to rivers, lakes and oceans
Run off
Ocean

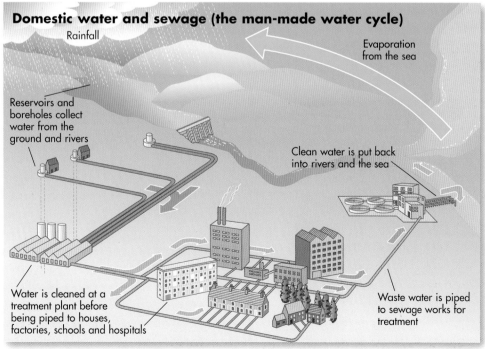

Domestic water and sewage (the man-made water cycle)

Rainfall
Evaporation from the sea
Reservoirs and boreholes collect water from the ground and rivers
Clean water is put back into rivers and the sea
Water is cleaned at a treatment plant before being piped to houses, factories, schools and hospitals
Waste water is piped to sewage works for treatment

Farming and fishing

Types of farm in the UK and Ireland

Dairy farms
Cows for milk, butter and cheese

Beef farms
Cows and calves for beef and veal

Sheep farms
Sheep and lambs for wool and meat

Grain and root farms
Wheat, potatoes, sugar beet and oilseed rape

Mixed farms
Livestock and grain or roots

Market gardening
Vegetables, fruit and flowers

Forests

Big cities

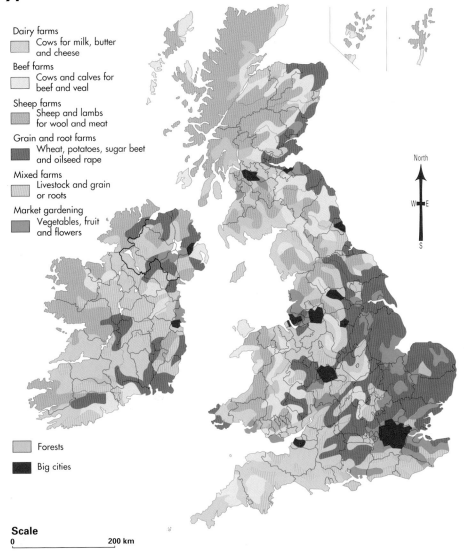

North
W E
S

Scale
0   200 km

Employment in agriculture

Percentage of the workforce employed in farming, forestry and fishing

Over 10%
2–10%
Under 10%

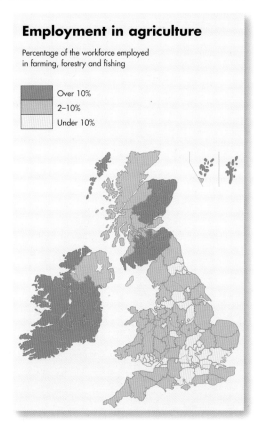

How much of our food is grown in the UK?

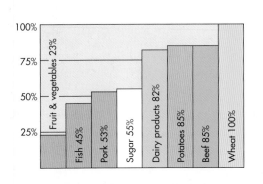

- Fruit & vegetables 23%
- Fish 45%
- Pork 53%
- Sugar 55%
- Dairy products 82%
- Potatoes 85%
- Beef 85%
- Wheat 100%

Where does the food eaten in the UK come from?

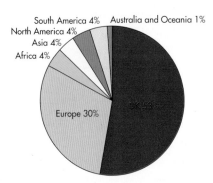

South America 4%   Australia and Oceania 1%
North America 4%
Asia 4%
Africa 4%
Europe 30%
UK 53%

Fishing

Large fishing ports (over 20,000 tonnes of fish caught each year)

Other important fishing ports

Scrabster
Kinlochbervie
Ullapool
Fraserburgh
Lerwick
Peterhead
Mallaig
ATLANTIC OCEAN
NORTH SEA
Killybegs
Kirkcudbright
North Shields
Portavogie
Kilkeel Ardglass Douglas
Rossaveel
Howth
IRISH SEA
Castletown Bearhaven
Dunmore East
Milford Haven
CELTIC SEA
Plymouth
Brixham
Shoreham
Newlyn
ENGLISH CHANNEL

Conservation

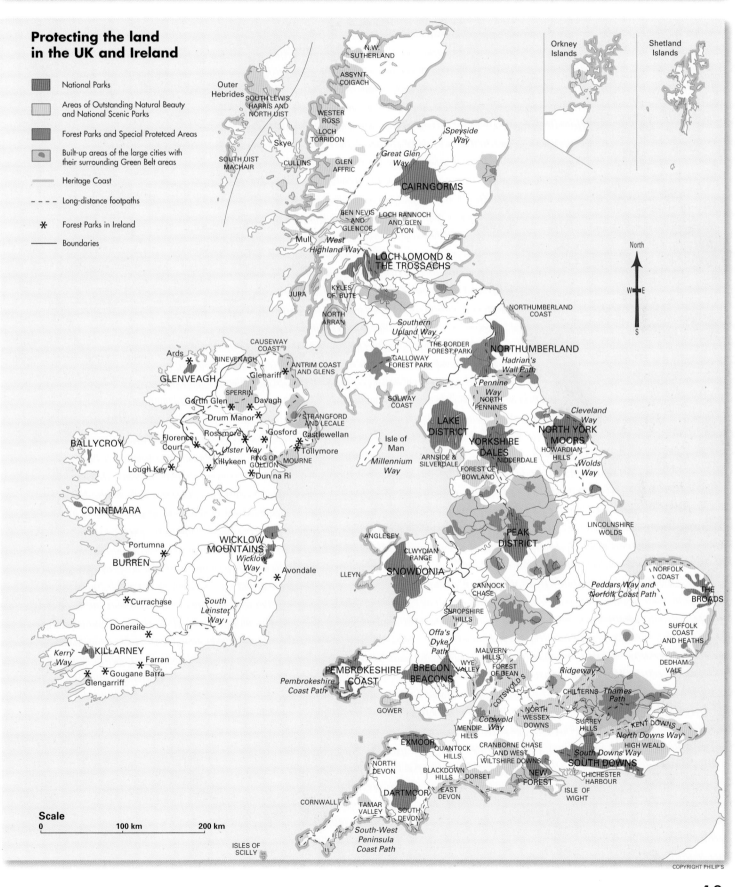

Protecting the land in the UK and Ireland

Legend:
- National Parks
- Areas of Outstanding Natural Beauty and National Scenic Parks
- Forest Parks and Special Protected Areas
- Built-up areas of the large cities with their surrounding Green Belt areas
- Heritage Coast
- - - - Long-distance footpaths
- * Forest Parks in Ireland
- Boundaries

Orkney Islands

Shetland Islands

N.W. SUTHERLAND
ASSYNT-COIGACH
Outer Hebrides
SOUTH LEWIS, HARRIS AND NORTH UIST
WESTER ROSS
Speyside Way
Great Glen Way
Skye
LOCH TORRIDON
GLEN AFFRIC
CAIRNGORMS
SOUTH UIST MACHAIR
CULLINS
BEN NEVIS AND GLENCOE
LOCH RANNOCH AND GLEN LYON
Mull
West Highland Way
LOCH LOMOND & THE TROSSACHS
JURA
KYLES OF BUTE
NORTH ARRAN
Southern Upland Way
NORTHUMBERLAND COAST

North
W E
S

CAUSEWAY COAST
Ards
BINEVENAGH
Glenariff
ANTRIM COAST AND GLENS
GLENVEAGH
SPERRIN
Gortin Glen
Davagh
Drum Manor
STRANGFORD AND LECALE
BALLYCROY
Florence Court
Rossmore
Gosford
Castlewellan
Killykeen
Ulster Way
RING OF GULLION
MOURNE
Tollymore
Lough Key
Dun na Ri
THE BORDER FOREST PARK
GALLOWAY FOREST PARK
SOLWAY COAST
NORTHUMBERLAND
Hadrian's Wall Path
Pennine Way
NORTH PENNINES
Cleveland Way
LAKE DISTRICT
YORKSHIRE DALES
NORTH YORK MOORS
HOWARDIAN HILLS
Wolds Way
Isle of Man
Millennium Way
ARNSIDE & SILVERDALE
NIDDERDALE
FOREST OF BOWLAND

CONNEMARA
Portumna
BURREN
WICKLOW MOUNTAINS
Wicklow Way
Avondale
ANGLESEY
LLEYN
CLWYDIAN RANGE
SNOWDONIA
PEAK DISTRICT
LINCOLNSHIRE WOLDS
Currachase
South Leinster Way
CANNOCK CHASE
SHROPSHIRE HILLS
Offa's Dyke Path
NORFOLK COAST
Peddars Way and Norfolk Coast Path
THE BROADS
SUFFOLK COAST AND HEATHS
Doneraile
Kerry Way
KILLARNEY
Farran
Gougane Barra
Glengarriff
PEMBROKESHIRE COAST
Pembrokeshire Coast Path
BRECON BEACONS
WYE VALLEY
MALVERN HILLS
FOREST OF DEAN
Ridgeway
DEDHAM VALE
COTSWOLDS
CHILTERNS
Thames Path
GOWER
NORTH WESSEX DOWNS
SURREY HILLS
KENT DOWNS
North Downs Way
Cotswold Way
MENDIP HILLS
CRANBORNE CHASE AND WEST WILTSHIRE DOWNS
HIGH WEALD
South Downs Way
SOUTH DOWNS
EXMOOR
QUANTOCK HILLS
CHICHESTER HARBOUR
NORTH DEVON
BLACKDOWN HILLS
DORSET
NEW FOREST
ISLE OF WIGHT
CORNWALL
DARTMOOR
EAST DEVON
TAMAR VALLEY
SOUTH DEVON
South-West Peninsula Coast Path
ISLES OF SCILLY

Scale

0   100 km   200 km

Work, industry and energy

Total workforce in the UK and Ireland

The number of people working

- Over 4 million
- 3–4 million
- 2–3 million
- Under 2 million

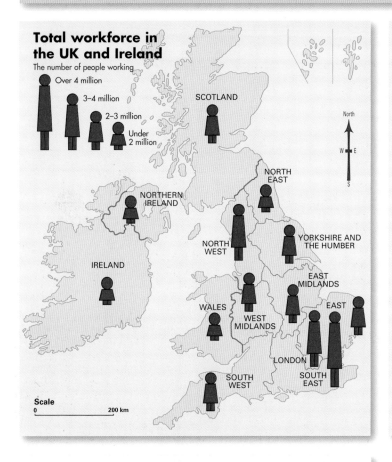

SCOTLAND

NORTHERN IRELAND

NORTH EAST

NORTH WEST

YORKSHIRE AND THE HUMBER

IRELAND

EAST MIDLANDS

WALES

WEST MIDLANDS

EAST

LONDON

SOUTH WEST

SOUTH EAST

North
W — E
S

Scale
0   200 km

Manufacturing industries are industries which make things. Some examples of manufactured goods are cars, steel, textiles and clothes.

Employment in service industries in the UK and Ireland

- Over 90%
- 80%–90%
- Under 80%

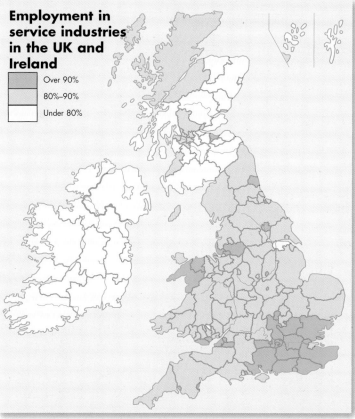

Service industries do not make things. They provide a service to people. Shops, hotels and banks are examples of service industries.

Unemployment

Percentage of the workforce unemployed

- Under 8%
- 8–10%
- Over 10%

Employment in manufacturing

Percentage of the workforce employed in manufacturing

- Under 10%
- 10–15%
- Over 15%

Income

The average amount each person earns each week

- Under £450
- £450–£500
- Over £500

No comparable data

14

Sources of energy used in the UK

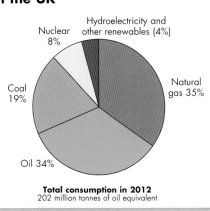

Hydroelectricity and other renewables (4%)

Nuclear 8%

Natural gas 35%

Coal 19%

Oil 34%

Total consumption in 2012
202 million tonnes of oil equivalent

Electricity generation in the UK (1990–2010)

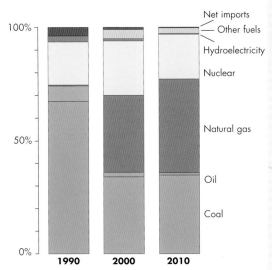

Net imports
Other fuels
Hydroelectricity
Nuclear
Natural gas
Oil
Coal

100%

50%

0%

1990 2000 2010

This bar-chart shows the different types of fuel that are used to make electricity in the UK. The use of coal and oil in the generation of electricity has dropped between 1990 and 2010. However, the use of natural gas has greatly increased.

Renewable energy in the UK

Renewable sources used to generate electricity (in million tonnes of oil equivalent)

	2002	2006	2009	2012
Biofuels	1.3	2.1	1.8	3.2
Hydroelectricity	1.1	1.0	1.2	1.2
Wind power	0.1	0.1	0.1	0.2
Solar	0	0	0	0.1
Other	0	0.8	2.6	6.0
Total renewables	2.5	4.0	5.7	10.7

In 2012 5.3% of electricity in the UK was generated by renewable energy sources. This is short of the government's target to increase this to 20% by 2020.

Energy sources in the UK and Ireland

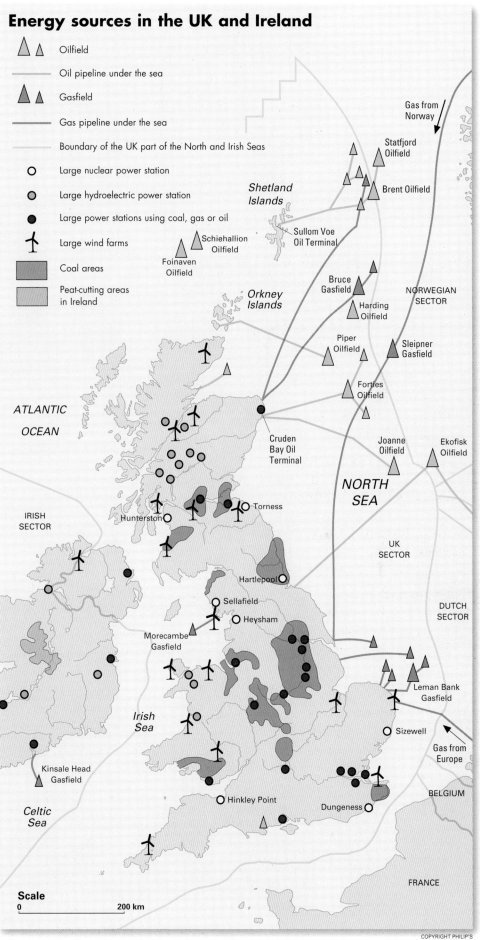

Oilfield

Oil pipeline under the sea

Gasfield

Gas pipeline under the sea

Boundary of the UK part of the North and Irish Seas

○ Large nuclear power station

◐ Large hydroelectric power station

● Large power stations using coal, gas or oil

✗ Large wind farms

▇ Coal areas

▢ Peat-cutting areas in Ireland

Gas from Norway

Statfjord Oilfield

Shetland Islands

Brent Oilfield

Sullom Voe Oil Terminal

Schiehallion Oilfield

Foinaven Oilfield

Bruce Gasfield

NORWEGIAN SECTOR

Orkney Islands

Harding Oilfield

Piper Oilfield

Sleipner Gasfield

ATLANTIC OCEAN

Forties Oilfield

Joanne Oilfield

Ekofisk Oilfield

NORTH SEA

Cruden Bay Oil Terminal

Torness

IRISH SECTOR

Hunterston

UK SECTOR

Hartlepool

DUTCH SECTOR

Sellafield

Heysham

Morecambe Gasfield

Leman Bank Gasfield

Irish Sea

Sizewell

Gas from Europe

Kinsale Head Gasfield

Celtic Sea

Hinkley Point

Dungeness

BELGIUM

FRANCE

Scale

0   200 km

COPYRIGHT PHILIP'S

Transport

There are about 407 thousand kilometres of road in the UK. The total number of cars, buses, lorries and motorbikes is 35 million. That is more than half the number of people in the UK. The maps on this page show the motorways and some main roads in the UK and the number of cars in the different regions. At the bottom of the page there are tables showing the road distances between important towns.

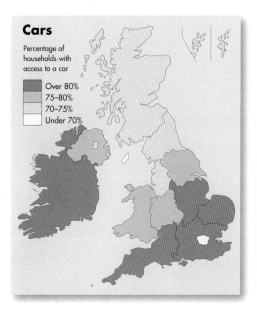

Cars

Percentage of households with access to a car

- Over 80%
- 75–80%
- 70–75%
- Under 70%

Roads in the UK and Ireland

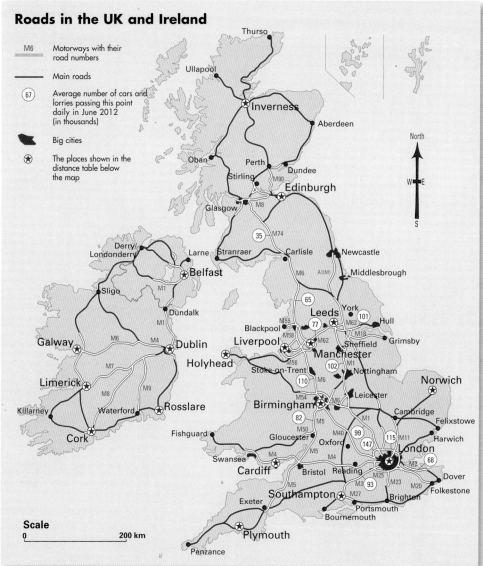

M6 — Motorways with their road numbers

— Main roads

(67) — Average number of cars and lorries passing this point daily in June 2012 (in thousands)

◤ — Big cities

✪ — The places shown in the distance table below the map

Scale
0 _____ 200 km

Road distances

The distance tables are in kilometres, but distances on road signposts in the UK are in miles.
A mile is longer than a kilometre.
1 mile = 1.6 kilometres. 1 kilometre = 0.6 mile.

UK	Birmingham	Cardiff	Edinburgh	Holyhead	Inverness	Leeds	Liverpool	London	Manchester	Norwich	Plymouth	Southampton
Birmingham		163	460	246	716	179	151	179	130	249	320	206
Cardiff	163		587	341	843	341	264	249	277	381	259	192
Edinburgh	460	587		489	256	320	338	608	336	586	790	669
Holyhead	246	341	489		745	262	151	420	198	481	528	455
Inverness	716	843	256	745		579	605	864	604	842	1049	925
Leeds	179	341	320	262	579		119	306	64	277	502	378
Liverpool	151	264	338	151	605	119		330	55	360	452	357
London	179	249	608	420	864	306	330		309	172	343	127
Manchester	130	277	336	198	604	64	55	309		306	457	325
Norwich	249	381	586	481	842	277	360	172	306		515	299
Plymouth	320	259	790	528	1049	502	452	343	457	515		246
Southampton	206	192	669	455	925	378	357	127	325	299	246	

Ireland	Belfast	Cork	Dublin	Galway	Limerick	Rosslare
Belfast		418	160	300	222	306
Cork	418		257	193	97	190
Dublin	160	257		210	193	137
Galway	300	193	210		97	249
Limerick	222	97	193	97		193
Rosslare	306	190	137	249	193	

Railways

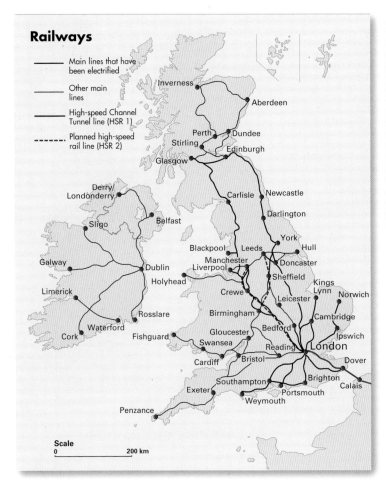

- Main lines that have been electrified
- Other main lines
- High-speed Channel Tunnel line (HSR 1)
- Planned high-speed rail line (HSR 2)

Scale
0 — 200 km

Manchester – the daily flow of cars

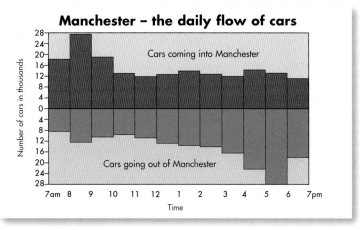

Cars coming into Manchester

Cars going out of Manchester

Number of cars in thousands

Time: 7am 8 9 10 11 12 1 2 3 4 5 6 7pm

High-speed rail

High-speed rail lines in Europe are shown in red on the map. Trains can travel at over 200 km/h on these lines.

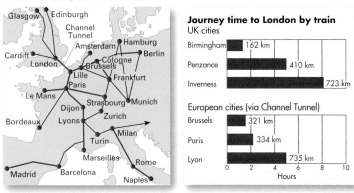

Journey time to London by train

UK cities
- Birmingham — 162 km
- Penzance — 410 km
- Inverness — 723 km

European cities (via Channel Tunnel)
- Brussels — 321 km
- Paris — 334 km
- Lyon — 735 km

Hours: 0 2 4 6 8 10

Ports and ferries

- Major ports
- Other ports
- Passenger ferries

Scale
0 — 200 km

Airports

- Over half the people are travelling within the UK or Ireland (Domestic airports)
- Over half the people are travelling to other countries (International airports)

Scale
0 — 200 km

Countries, regions and counties

Country names

The map on the left shows the **British Isles**, which is made up of the two large islands of **Great Britain** and **Ireland** and many smaller islands. The islands contain two countries, the **United Kingdom** and **Ireland**. The full name of the United Kingdom is The United Kingdom of Great Britain and Northern Ireland. It has four parts: **England**, **Wales**, **Scotland** and **Northern Ireland**. It is known for short as the United Kingdom, UK or Britain. The whole country is often wrongly called England. Ireland is sometimes shown as Eire (on its stamps), which is the name of Ireland in the Irish language.

Countries and regions

The map shows the Standard Regions of the United Kingdom. The boundaries follow those of the counties shown on page 19. Large bodies like the Health Service and Water and Power providers divide the country up into their own regions. Ireland is divided into four historic provinces.

Counties and unitary authorities

England and Wales are divided into counties, unitary authorities and boroughs.

Scotland is divided into regions and unitary authorities, and Northern Ireland into districts.

Ireland is divided into counties.

Area data	
	Area in square kilometres
England	130,439
Wales	20,768
Scotland	77,167
Northern Ireland	13,483
United Kingdom	**241,857**
Isle of Man	**572**
Channel Islands	**195**
Ireland	**68,896**

Counties and Unitary Authorities of the UK and Ireland

Authorities which are too small to name on the map are numbered and listed separately.

SCOTLAND
1. ABERDEEN CITY
2. DUNDEE CITY
3. WEST DUNBARTONSHIRE
4. EAST DUNBARTONSHIRE
5. CITY OF GLASGOW
6. INVERCLYDE
7. RENFREWSHIRE
8. EAST RENFREWSHIRE
9. NORTH LANARKSHIRE
10. FALKIRK
11. CLACKMANNANSHIRE
12. WEST LOTHIAN
13. CITY OF EDINBURGH
14. MIDLOTHIAN

WALES
15. SWANSEA
16. NEATH PORT TALBOT
17. BRIDGEND
18. RHONDDA CYNON TAFF
19. MERTHYR TYDFIL
20. CAERPHILLY
21. BLAENAU GWENT
22. TORFAEN
23. CARDIFF
24. NEWPORT

The Channel Islands and the Isle of Man are dependencies of the Crown and have their own parliaments. They are not part of the United Kingdom.

ENGLAND
25. HARTLEPOOL
26. DARLINGTON
27. STOCKTON-ON-TEES
28. MIDDLESBROUGH
29. REDCAR AND CLEVELAND
30. BLACKPOOL
31. BLACKBURN WITH DARWEN
32. HALTON
33. WARRINGTON
34. KINGSTON UPON HULL
35. NORTH EAST LINCOLNSHIRE
36. STOKE-ON-TRENT
37. TELFORD AND WREKIN
38. DERBY CITY
39. CITY OF NOTTINGHAM
40. LEICESTER CITY
41. RUTLAND
42. PETERBOROUGH
43. MILTON KEYNES
44. LUTON
45. NORTH SOMERSET
46. CITY OF BRISTOL
47. BATH AND N. E. SOMERSET
48. SWINDON
49. READING
50. WOKINGHAM
51. WINDSOR AND MAIDENHEAD
52. SLOUGH
53. BRACKNELL FOREST
54. THURROCK
55. SOUTHEND-ON-SEA
56. MEDWAY
57. PLYMOUTH
58. TORBAY
59. POOLE
60. BOURNEMOUTH
61. SOUTHAMPTON
62. PORTSMOUTH
63. BRIGHTON AND HOVE
64. CHESHIRE WEST AND CHESTER
65. CHESHIRE EAST
66. BEDFORD
67. CENTRAL BEDFORDSHIRE

Capital cities

Scale

0   100 km   200 km

COPYRIGHT PHILIP'S

People, cities and towns

Old people and young people

 In these counties, young people are a large group in the population (over 20%). On this map young people are those aged under 15 years old.

 In these counties, old people are a large group in the population (over 20%). On this map old people are those aged over 65 years old.

Look at the colours on the map above. Can you think of some reasons why some counties have more older people than others?

People in the UK and Ireland

Number of people per square kilometre in 2011

- Over 500 – very high density
- 100–500 – high density
- 50–100 – medium density
- Under 50 – low density

The average density for the UK is 261 people per square km.

The average density for Ireland is 67 people per square km.

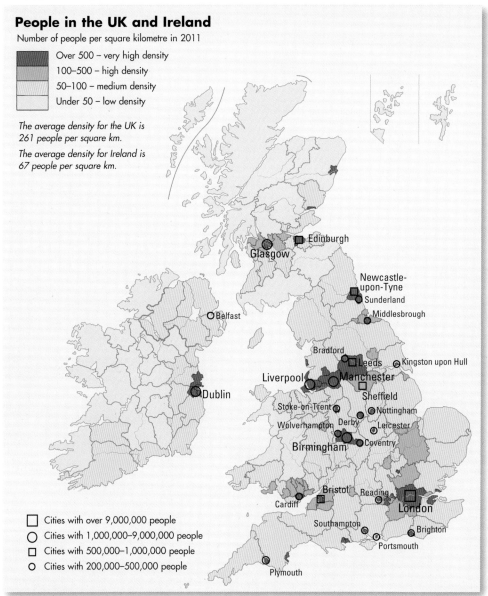

- ☐ Cities with over 9,000,000 people
- ○ Cities with 1,000,000–9,000,000 people
- ▫ Cities with 500,000–1,000,000 people
- ◦ Cities with 200,000–500,000 people

Country population data

	1901	1951	2013
	millions		
England	30.5	41.2	53.9
Wales	2.0	2.6	3.1
Scotland	4.5	5.1	5.3
Northern Ireland	1.2	1.4	1.8
United Kingdom	**38.2**	**50.3**	**64.1**
Ireland	**3.2**	**2.9**	**4.8**

Changing numbers

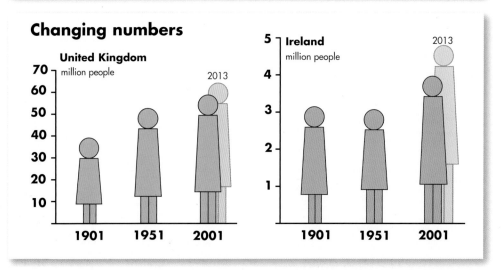

Cities and towns of the UK and Ireland

Map scale

This distance is 400 kilometres

0   400 km

Map information

Height of land

metres
Over 1,000
500–1,000
200–500
0–200
Below sea level
Sea

Cities and towns

London ■ Over 9,000,000 people
Dublin ■ 1,000,000 - 9,000,000 people
Leeds ● 500,000 – 1,000,000 people
Plymouth ● 200,000 – 500,000 people
Oxford ● 100,000 – 200,000 people
Guildford ● 50,000 – 100,000 people
Dover • Under 50,000 people

North

W E
S

Shetland Islands
Lerwick

Orkney Islands
Kirkwall

Thurso
Wick
Helmsdale
Stornoway
Ullapool
Lairg
Golspie
Invergordon
Dingwall
Nairn
Elgin
Banff
Fraserburgh
Inverness
Huntly
Peterhead
Inverurie
Portree
Aviemore
Aberdeen
Mallaig
SCOTLAND
Stonehaven
Fort William
Ballater
Tobermory
Montrose
Oban
Forfar
Arbroath
Perth
Dundee
St. Andrews
Stirling
Glenrothes
Dunfermline
Kirkcaldy
Dumbarton
Dunbar
Greenock
Glasgow
Paisley
Edinburgh
East Kilbride
Hamilton
Berwick-upon-Tweed
Irvine
Galashiels
Kilmarnock
Jedburgh
Campbeltown
Ayr
Hawick
Alnwick

Outer Hebrides
Inner Hebrides

ATLANTIC OCEAN

North Sea

Buncrana
Coleraine
Letterkenny
Ballymena
Larne
Derry/Londonderry
Donegal
NORTHERN IRELAND
Antrim
Bangor
Bundoran
Omagh
Portadown
Belfast
Lisburn
Ballina
Sligo
Enniskillen
Lurgan
Armagh
Newry
Castlebar
Cavan
Westport
Roscommon
Longford
Dundalk
Drogheda
Athlone
Mullingar
Galway
Ballinasloe
Tullamore
IRELAND
Birr
Ennis
Portlaoise
Dublin
Dun Laoghaire
Nenagh
Carlow
Bray
Limerick
Thurles
Kilkenny
Arklow
Tipperary
Clonmel
Carrick-on-Suir
Wexford
Tralee
Waterford
Rosslare Harbour
Dingle
Mallow
Dungarvan
Killarney
Cork
Youghal
Bantry
Bandon
Cóbh

Stranraer
Girvan
Dumfries
Workington
Carlisle
Whitehaven
Newcastle-upon-Tyne
South Shields
Gateshead
Sunderland
Durham
Hartlepool
Darlington
Redcar
Middlesbrough
Stockton
Barrow-in-Furness
Scarborough
Lancaster
Harrogate
Bridlington
Douglas
Isle of Man
UNITED
KINGDOM
York
Leeds
Kingston upon Hull
Blackpool
Keighley
Burnley
Bradford
Preston
Halifax
Huddersfield
Scunthorpe
Blackburn
Bolton
Barnsley
Grimsby
Manchester
Oldham
Doncaster
Liverpool
Stockport
Sheffield
Rotherham
Warrington
Chesterfield
Lincoln
Louth
Chester
Mansfield
Skegness
Crewe
Boston
Bangor
Wrexham
Stoke-on-Trent
Derby
Nottingham
Cromer
Pwllheli
Stafford
Grantham
King's Lynn
Great Yarmouth
Shrewsbury
Telford
ENGLAND
Norwich
Welshpool
Nuneaton
Leicester
Peterborough
Thetford
Lowestoft
Aberystwyth
Wolverhampton
Corby
Ely
Birmingham
Coventry
Rugby
Cambridge
Bury St. Edmunds
Ipswich
Worcester
Northampton
Felixstowe
Hereford
Milton Keynes
Bedford
Harwich
Fishguard
Brecon
Cheltenham
Stevenage
Colchester
Haverfordwest
Carmarthen
Oxford
Luton
Harlow
Chelmsford
Milford Haven
Merthyr Tydfil
Gloucester
Watford
Basildon
Pembroke
Neath
Cwmbran
High Wycombe
Slough
Southend
Llanelli
Rhondda
Newport
Swindon
London
Margate
Swansea
Cardiff
Bristol
Reading
Chatham
Port Talbot
Barry
Bath
Newbury
Basingstoke
Reigate
Maidstone
Canterbury
Dover
WALES
Weston-super-Mare
Guildford
Ashford
Folkestone
Barnstaple
Salisbury
Winchester
Crawley
Taunton
Hastings
Bude
Yeovil
Southampton
Havant
Eastbourne
Boulogne-sur-Mer
Exeter
Bournemouth
Portsmouth
Brighton
Worthing
Exmouth
Poole
Newport
Calais
Newquay
Torquay
Weymouth
Truro
St. Austell
Plymouth
FRANCE
Falmouth
Penzance

Irish Sea
Holyhead

Celtic Sea

West from Greenwich   East from Greenwich

COPYRIGHT PHILIP'S

21

Tourism

Tourism in the UK and Ireland

- ● Main holiday destinations
- ○ Other major tourist attractions

Inverness, Nairn, Loch Ness, Aviemore, Fort William, Montrose, Oban, Arbroath, Dunoon, Dunbar, Glasgow, Edinburgh, Giant's Causeway, Ayr, Portrush, Hadrian's Wall, Bundoran, Bangor, Sligo, Windermere, Fountains Abbey, Whitby, Lough Key Nature Park, Scarborough, Killykeen Forest Park, Douglas, Morecambe, Flamingo Land, Bridlington, Knock Shrine, Blackpool, York, Xscape, Galway, Tayto Park, Southport, Saltaire, DUBLIN, Llandudno, Manchester, Liverpool, Derwent Valley Mills, Skegness, Cliffs of Moher, Powerscourt Castle, Bray, Gwynedd Castles, Chester, Alton Towers, Kilkee, Great Yarmouth, Limerick, Arklow, Ironbridge Gorge, Drayton Manor, Thetford Forest Park, Bunratty Castle, Aberystwyth, Stratford-upon-Avon, Fairlands Valley Park, Lee Valley Regional Park, Clacton, Blarney Castle, Blenheim, Killarney, Cork, Fota Wildlife Park, Tenby, Blaenavon, Legoland Windsor, LONDON, Southend, Bath, Greenwich, Margate, Thorpe Park, Chessington, Canterbury, Weston-super-Mare, Brighton, Minehead, Stonehenge, Worthing, Hastings, Eastbourne, Bournemouth, Newquay, Torbay, Weymouth, St. Ives, Eden Project

North W E S

Scale 0 — 200 km

Tourist traffic

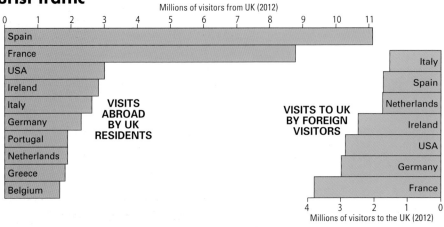

Millions of visitors from UK (2012)
0 1 2 3 4 5 6 7 8 9 10 11

- Spain
- France
- USA
- Ireland
- Italy
- Germany
- Portugal
- Netherlands
- Greece
- Belgium

VISITS ABROAD BY UK RESIDENTS

VISITS TO UK BY FOREIGN VISITORS

- Italy
- Spain
- Netherlands
- Ireland
- USA
- Germany
- France

4 3 2 1 0
Millions of visitors to the UK (2012)

UK tourist attractions

(number of visitors in millions, 2012)

1.	British Museum, London	5.6
2.	Tate Modern, London	5.3
3.	National Gallery, London	5.2
4.	Natural History Museum, London	5.0
5.	Victoria and Albert Museum, London	3.2
6.	Science Museum, London	3.0
7.	Tower of London	2.4
8.	National Portrait Gallery, London	2.1
9.	National Museum of Scotland, Edinburgh	1.9
10.	St Paul's Cathedral, London	1.8
11.	Old Royal Naval College, Greenwich	1.8
12.	Westminster Abbey, London	1.8
13.	Tate Britain, London	1.5
14.	British Library, London	1.4
15.	Chester Zoo	1.4
16.	Edinburgh Castle	1.2
17.	Royal Academy of Arts, London	1.2
18.	National Maritime Museum, Greenwich	1.1
19.	Roman Baths and Pump Room, Bath	1.1
20.	Stonehenge, Wiltshire	1.0

Ireland tourist attractions

(number of visitors in millions, 2012)

1.	Guinness Storehouse, Dublin	1.1
2.	Dublin Zoo	1.0
3.	Cliffs of Moher, Clare	0.9
4.	National Aquatic Centre, Dublin	0.8
5.	National Gallery, Dublin	0.7
6.	Book of Kells, Dublin	0.6
7.	National Botanic Gardens, Dublin	0.5
8.	Tayto Park, Meath	0.4
9.	St Patrick's Cathedral, Dublin	0.4
10.	Fota Wildlife Park, Cork	0.4

World tourist attractions

(number of foreign visitors in millions, 2012)

1.	France	83.0
2.	USA	67.0
3.	China	57.7
4.	Spain	57.7
5.	Italy	46.4
6.	Saudi Arabia	43.7
7.	Germany	30.4
8.	UK	29.3
9.	Russia	25.7
10.	Malaysia	25.0
11.	Austria	24.2
12.	Hong Kong	23.8
13.	Mexico	23.4
14.	Ukraine	23.0
15.	Thailand	22.4

International organizations

United Nations

The UN is the largest international organization in the world. The headquarters are in New York and 193 countries are members. It was formed in 1945 to help solve world problems and to help keep world peace. The UN sends peacekeeping forces to areas where there are problems.

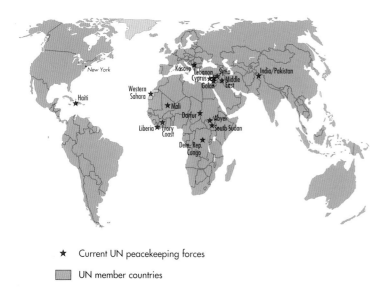

★ Current UN peacekeeping forces

▨ UN member countries

Population (million people)

Austria	8
Belgium	10
Bulgaria	7
Croatia	4
Cyprus	1
Czech Republic	11
Denmark	6
Estonia	1
Finland	5
France	66
Germany	81
Greece	11
Hungary	10
Ireland	5
Italy	62
Latvia	2
Lithuania	4
Luxembourg	0.5
Malta	0.4
Netherlands	17
Poland	38
Portugal	11
Romania	22
Slovak Republic	5
Slovenia	2
Spain	48
Sweden	10
UK	64

European Union

▨ EU member countries

The EU was first formed in 1951. Six countries were members. Now there are 28 countries in the EU. These countries meet to discuss agriculture, industry and trade as well as social and political issues. The headquarters are in Brussels. Cyprus, the Czech Republic, Estonia, Hungary, Latvia, Lithuania, Malta, Poland, the Slovak Republic and Slovenia joined the EU in 2004. Bulgaria and Romania joined in 2007, Croatia in 2013.

The Commonwealth

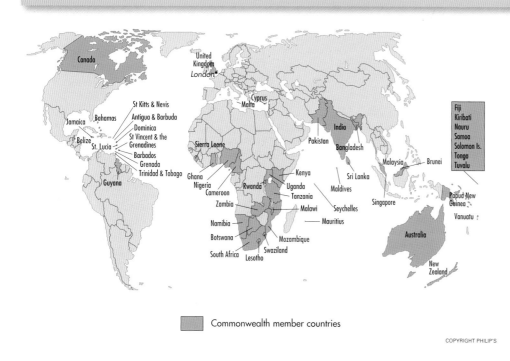

▨ Commonwealth member countries

The Commonwealth is a group of 54 independent countries which used to belong to the British Empire. It is organized by a group of people called the Secretariat which is based in London. Queen Elizabeth II is the head of the Commonwealth. About every two years the heads of the different governments meet to discuss world problems. These meetings are held in different countries in the Commonwealth.

England and Wales

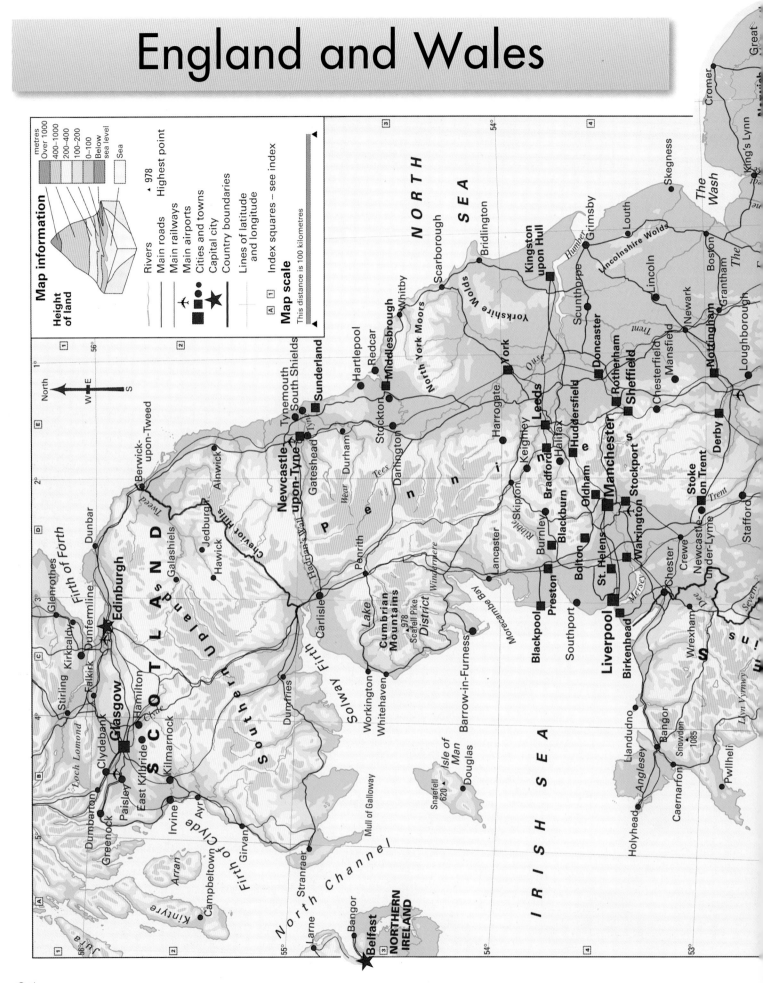

Map information

Height of land

metres	
Over 1000	
400–1000	
200–400	
100–200	
0–100	
Below sea level	
Sea	

▲ 978 Highest point

Rivers
Main roads
Main railways
✈ Main airports
● Cities and towns
★ Capital city
Country boundaries
Lines of latitude and longitude

A 1 Index squares – see index

Map scale

This distance is 100 kilometres

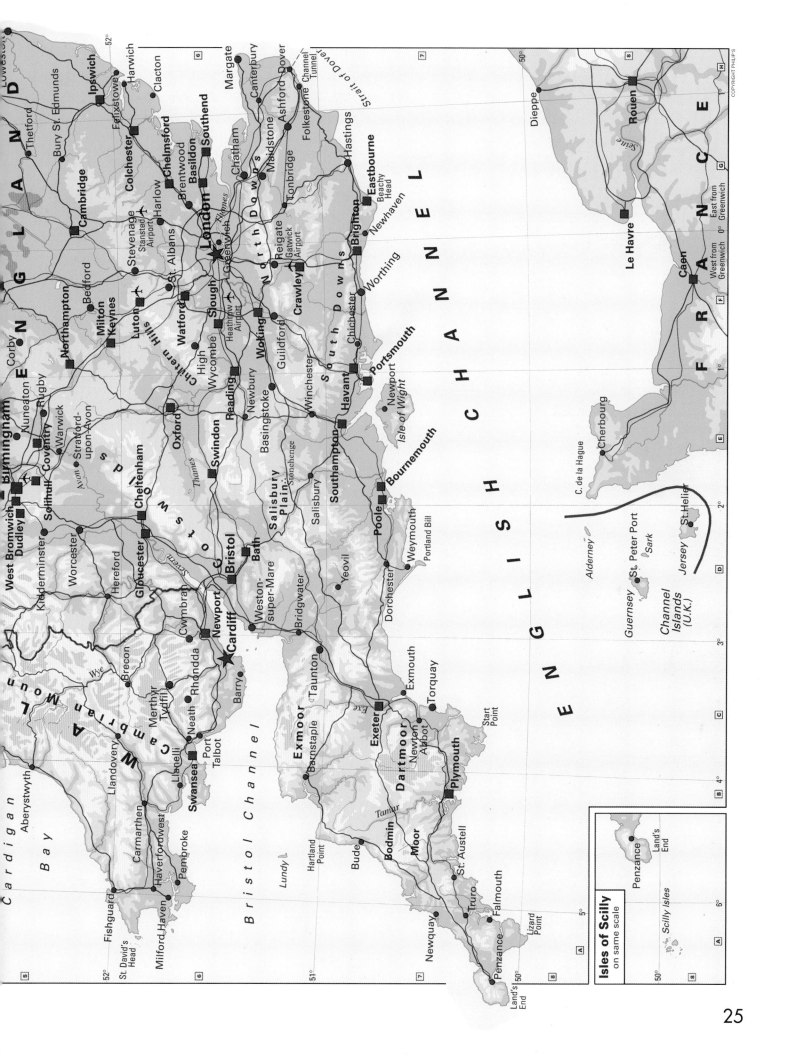

25

Isles of Scilly
on same scale

Scotland and Ireland

Orkney Islands
on same scale

Westray · Sanday
Rousay · Stronsay
Mainland
59°
Kirkwall
Hoy · South Ronaldsay
Pentland Firth
John o' Groats · 3°

Shetland Islands
on same scale

Unst
Yell · Fetlar
Sullom Voe
Mainland
Lerwick
Foula

NORTHERN IRELAND
Larne
Carrickfergus
Stranraer

Cape Wrath · Thurso · John o' Groats
Wick
Helmsdale
Lairg · Golspie
Ullapool
Invergordon
Stornoway
Lewis
Harris
Outer Hebrides
Inner Hebrides
North Uist
Benbecula
South Uist
Barra
Portree
Skye
Rhum
Eigg
Coll
Tobermory
Tiree
Staffa
Iona
Mull
Colonsay
Jura
Islay
Kintyre
Arran
Bute
Campbeltown
Mull of Kintyre

North West Highlands
Dingwall
Kyle of Lochalsh
Mallaig
Fort William
Ben Nevis 1344
Glen Coe
Oban
Loch Awe
Crianlarich
Loch Lomond
Dumbarton
Greenock
Paisley
Clydebank
Glasgow
East Kilbride
Irvine
Troon
Ayr
Kilmarnock
Girvan

Elgin · Banff · Fraserburgh
Keith · Peterhead
Nairn · Huntly
Inverness · Inverurie · Dyce
Spey · **Aberdeen**
Westhill
Aviemore · Don
Cairn Gorm 1245 · Dee
Ballater · Stonehaven
Grampian Mountains
Pitlochry · Montrose
Forfar
Arbroath
Dundee
Perth · St. Andrews
Callander · Glenrothes
Stirling · Kirkcaldy · Firth of Forth
Cumbernauld · Dunfermline · Dunbar
Falkirk
Hamilton
Edinburgh
Berwick-upon-Tweed
Galashiels
Jedburgh · Alnwick
Hawick · Cheviot Hills
Southern Uplands
Lockerbie
Dumfries · Hadrian's Wall · Hexham
Carlisle · **ENGLAND**
Wear

Loch Ness
Glen Mor
Moray Firth
Tay
Loch Fyne
Firth of Clyde
North Channel
Solway Firth
Tweed

ATLANTIC OCEAN
NORTH SEA

Map scale
This distance is 100 kilometres

COPYRIGHT PHILIP'S

26

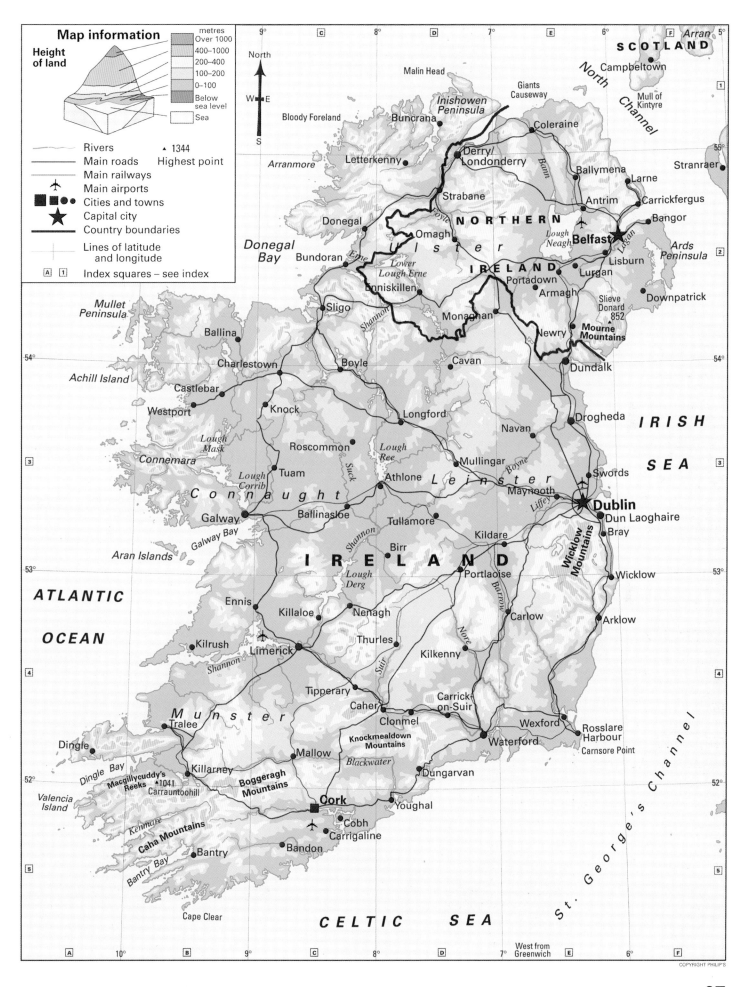

Map information

Height of land

	metres
	Over 1000
	400–1000
	200–400
	100–200
	0–100
	Below sea level
	Sea

Rivers
Main roads
Main railways
✈ Main airports
■ ■ ● ● Cities and towns
★ Capital city
Country boundaries
Lines of latitude and longitude
A 1 Index squares – see index

▲ 1344 Highest point

North
W—E
S

SCOTLAND
Campbeltown
Mull of Kintyre
Arran
North Channel
Stranraer
Larne
Carrickfergus
Bangor
Ards Peninsula
Downpatrick

Malin Head
Giants Causeway
Coleraine
Ballymena
Antrim
Belfast
Lisburn
Lurgan
Portadown
Armagh
Newry
Slieve Donard 852
Mourne Mountains
Dundalk

Inishowen Peninsula
Buncrana
Bloody Foreland
Letterkenny
Derry/Londonderry
Strabane
Donegal
Omagh
Arranmore
NORTHERN
U l s t e r
I R E L A N D
Lough Neagh
Bann
Foyle
Monaghan
Cavan

Donegal Bay
Bundoran
Enniskillen
Lower Lough Erne
Erne
Sligo
Boyle
Longford

Mullet Peninsula
Ballina
Charlestown
Castlebar
Westport
Knock
Achill Island
Shannon

Lough Mask
Connemara
Lough Corrib
Tuam
Roscommon
Lough Ree
Athlone
Stuck

C o n n a u g h t
Galway
Ballinasloe
Galway Bay
Aran Islands

ATLANTIC OCEAN

Navan
Drogheda
Swords
Maynooth
Dublin
Dun Laoghaire
Bray
Mullingar
Boyne
L e i n s t e r
Liffey

I R E L A N D
Tullamore
Kildare
Birr
Portlaoise
Wicklow Mountains
Wicklow
Shannon
Lough Derg
Barrow

Ennis
Killaloe
Nenagh
Carlow
Arklow
Kilrush
Limerick
Thurles
Kilkenny
Nore

Shannon
Tipperary
Caher
Carrick-on-Suir
Wexford
Rosslare Harbour
Carnsore Point

M u n s t e r
Tralee
Clonmel
Waterford
Dungarvan
Knockmealdown Mountains
Suir
Dingle
Mallow
Blackwater
Youghal
Dingle Bay
Killarney
Boggeragh Mountains
Macgillycuddy's Reeks ▲1041
Carrauntoohill
Cork
Cobh
Carrigaline
Valencia Island
Caha Mountains
Bantry
Bandon
Kenmare
Bantry Bay
Cape Clear

IRISH SEA

CELTIC SEA

St. George's Channel

West from Greenwich

COPYRIGHT PHILIP'S

27

The Earth as a planet

Relative sizes of the planets

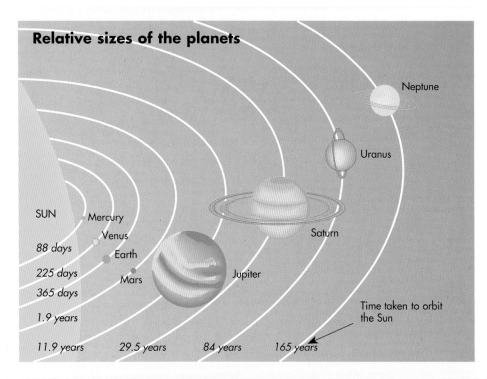

SUN

Mercury
Venus
Earth
Mars
Jupiter
Saturn
Uranus
Neptune

88 days
225 days
365 days
1.9 years
11.9 years   29.5 years   84 years   165 years

Time taken to orbit the Sun

The Solar System

The Earth is one of the eight planets that orbit the Sun. These two diagrams show how big the planets are, how far they are away from the Sun and how long they take to orbit the Sun. The diagram on the left shows how the planets closest to the Sun have the shortest orbits. The Earth takes 365 days (a year) to go round the Sun. The Earth is the fifth largest planet. It is much smaller than Jupiter and Saturn which are the largest planets.

Distances of the planets from the Sun in millions of kilometres

Mercury 58
Venus 108
Earth 150
Mars 228
Jupiter 778
Saturn 1,430
Uranus 2,870
Neptune 4,500

Planet Earth

The Earth spins as if it is on a rod – its axis. The axis would come out of the Earth at two points. The northern point is called the North Pole and the southern point is called the South Pole. The distance between the Poles through the centre of the Earth is 12,700 km.

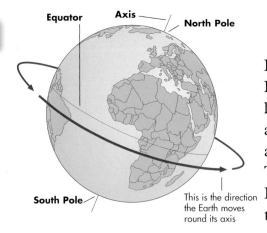

Equator   Axis   North Pole

South Pole

This is the direction the Earth moves round its axis

It takes a day (24 hours) for the Earth to rotate on its axis. It is light (day) when it faces the Sun and dark (night) when it faces away. See the diagram below. The Equator is a line round the Earth which is halfway between the Poles. It is 40,000 km long.

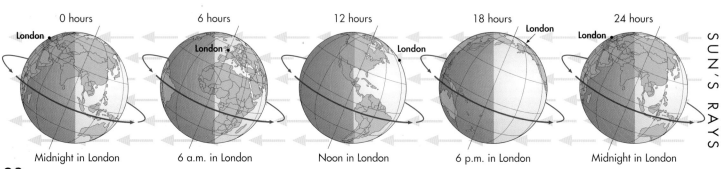

0 hours   6 hours   12 hours   18 hours   24 hours

London   London   London   London   London

Midnight in London   6 a.m. in London   Noon in London   6 p.m. in London   Midnight in London

SUN'S RAYS

28

The year and seasons

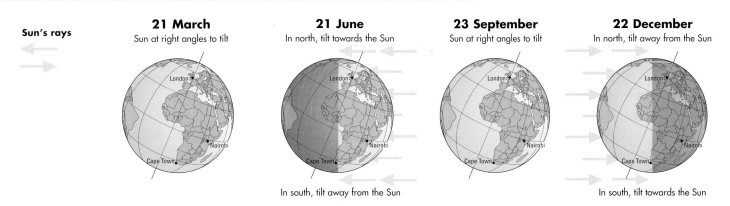

The Earth is always tilted at 66½°. It moves around the Sun. This movement gives us the seasons of the year. In June the northern hemisphere tilts towards the Sun so it is summer. Six months later, in December, the Earth has rotated halfway round the Sun. It is then summer in the southern hemisphere.

northern spring
southern autumn

21 MARCH

The Earth goes round the Sun. This takes 365 days.

northern summer

N

21 JUNE

S

southern winter

SUN

150 million km

northern winter

22 DECEMBER

southern summer

This is the direction the Earth moves round the Sun.

23 SEPTEMBER

northern autumn
southern spring

Sun's rays

21 March
Sun at right angles to tilt

21 June
In north, tilt towards the Sun

In south, tilt away from the Sun

23 September
Sun at right angles to tilt

22 December
In north, tilt away from the Sun

In south, tilt towards the Sun

Season	Northern spring Southern autumn			Northern summer Southern winter			Northern autumn Southern spring			Northern winter Southern summer		
City	London	Nairobi	CapeTown	London	Nairobi	CapeTown	London	Nairobi	CapeTown	London	Nairobi	CapeTown
Latitude	51°N	1°S	34°S	51°N	1°S	34°S	51°N	1°S	34°S	51°N	1°S	34°S
Day length	12 hrs	12 hrs	12 hrs	16 hrs	12 hrs	10 hrs	12 hrs	12 hrs	12 hrs	8 hrs	12 hrs	14 hrs
Night length	12 hrs	12 hrs	12 hrs	8 hrs	12 hrs	14 hrs	12 hrs	12 hrs	12 hrs	16 hrs	12 hrs	10 hrs
Temperature	7°C	21°C	21°C	16°C	18°C	13°C	15°C	19°C	14°C	5°C	19°C	20°C

The Moon

The Moon is about a quarter the size of the Earth. It orbits the Earth in just over 27 days (almost a month). The Moon is round but we on Earth see only the parts lit by the Sun. This makes it look as if the Moon is a different shape at different times of the month. These are known as the phases of the Moon and they are shown in this diagram.

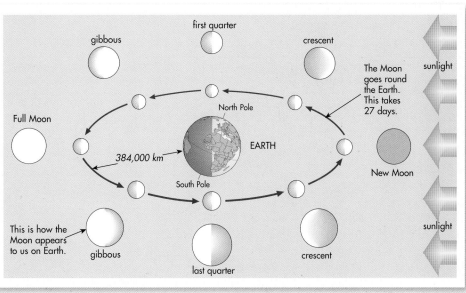

first quarter

gibbous

crescent

The Moon goes round the Earth. This takes 27 days.

sunlight

Full Moon

North Pole

384,000 km

EARTH

South Pole

New Moon

This is how the Moon appears to us on Earth.

gibbous

last quarter

crescent

sunlight

Mountains, seas and rivers

Over 70% of the surface of the Earth is covered with water and ice. Most of the mountain ranges have been formed by movements in the Earth's crust. They are coloured brown on the map. Rivers shape the landscape as they flow to the sea.

Largest oceans

(thousand square kilometres)

1. Pacific Ocean . . 155,557
2. Atlantic Ocean . . 76,762
3. Indian Ocean . . . 68,556
4. Southern Ocean . . 20,237
5. Arctic Ocean . . . 14,351

Largest seas

(thousand square kilometres)

1. Mediterranean Sea 2,966
2. South China Sea   2,318
3. Bering Sea 2,274
4. Caribbean Sea . . . 1,942
5. Gulf of Mexico . . . 1,813
6. Sea of Okhotsk . . . 1,528

Highest mountains

(metres)

Asia: Mt Everest 8,850
South America:
  Aconcagua 6,962
North America:
  Mt McKinley 6,168
Africa: Kilimanjaro . . 5,895
Europe: Elbrus 5,642

The course of a river

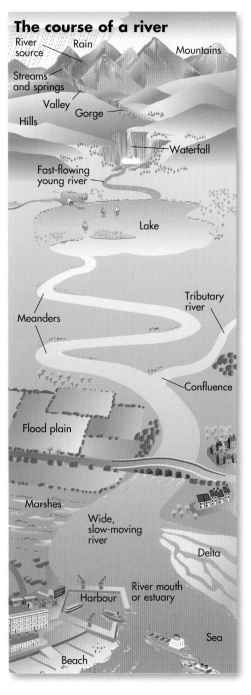

River source
Rain
Mountains
Streams and springs
Valley
Gorge
Hills
Waterfall
Fast-flowing young river
Lake
Tributary river
Meanders
Confluence
Flood plain
Marshes
Wide, slow-moving river
Delta
River mouth or estuary
Harbour
Sea
Beach

Largest lakes	Longest rivers	Largest islands	Deepest trenches
(thousand square kilometres)	(kilometres)	(thousand square kilometres)	(metres)
1. Caspian Sea 371	1. Nile 6,695	1. Greenland 2,176	1. Mariana Trench 11,022
2. Lake Superior. 82	2. Amazon 6,450	2. New Guinea. 821	2. Tonga Trench 10,822
3. Lake Victoria 68	3. Yangtse 6,380	3. Borneo. 744	3. Japan Trench 10,554
4. Lake Huron 60	4. Mississippi 5,971	4. Madagascar 587	4. Kuril Trench 10,542
5. Lake Michigan 58	5. Yenisey. 5,550	5. Baffin Island. 508	5. Mindanao Trench . .10,497
6. Lake Tanganyika 33	6. Hwang-Ho 5,464	6. Sumatra 474	6. Kermadec Trench . .10,047
7. Great Bear Lake 32	7. Ob 5,410	7. Honshu 231	7. Bougainville Trench . .9,140
8. Lake Baikal 31	8. Congo 4,670	8. Great Britain 230	8. Milwaukee Deep 8,605
9. Lake Malawi. 30	9. Mekong 4,500	9. Victoria Island 212	9. South Sandwich Trench 8,325
10. Great Salt Lake 29	10. Amur 4,442	10. Ellesmere Island 197	10. Aleutian Trench 7,822

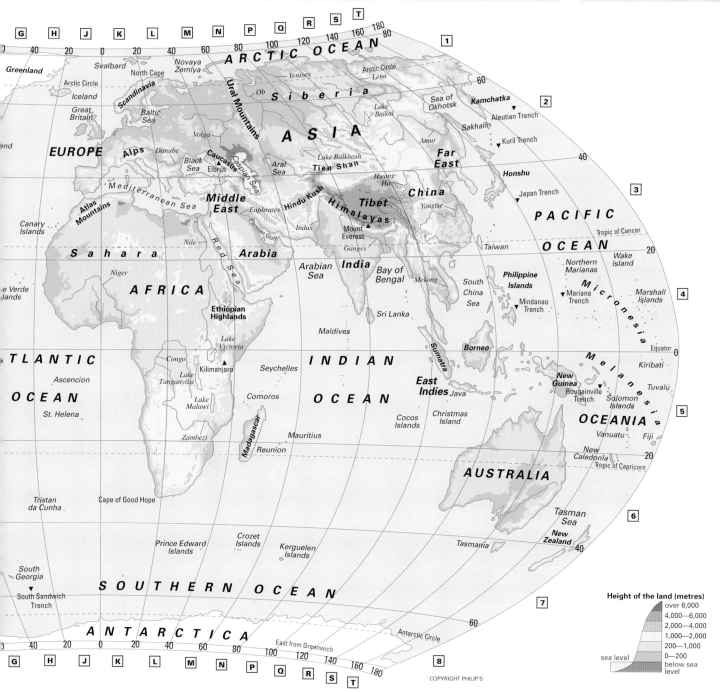

Height of the land (metres)
over 6,000
4,000—6,000
2,000—4,000
1,000—2,000
200—1,000
0—200
sea level
below sea level

COPYRIGHT PHILIP'S

31

Climate

Key to the climate map

Tropical climate (hot and wet)
Heavy rainfall and high temperatures all the year with little difference between the hot and cold months.

Dry climate (desert and steppe)
Many months, often years, without rain. High temperatures in the summer but cooler in winter.

Mild climate (warm and wet)
Rain every month. Warm summers and cool winters.

Continental climate (cold and wet)
Mild summers and very cold winters.

Polar climate (very cold and dry)
Very cold at all times, especially in the winter months. Very little rainfall.

Mountainous areas (where altitude affects climate type)
Lower temperatures because the land is high. Heavy rain and snow.

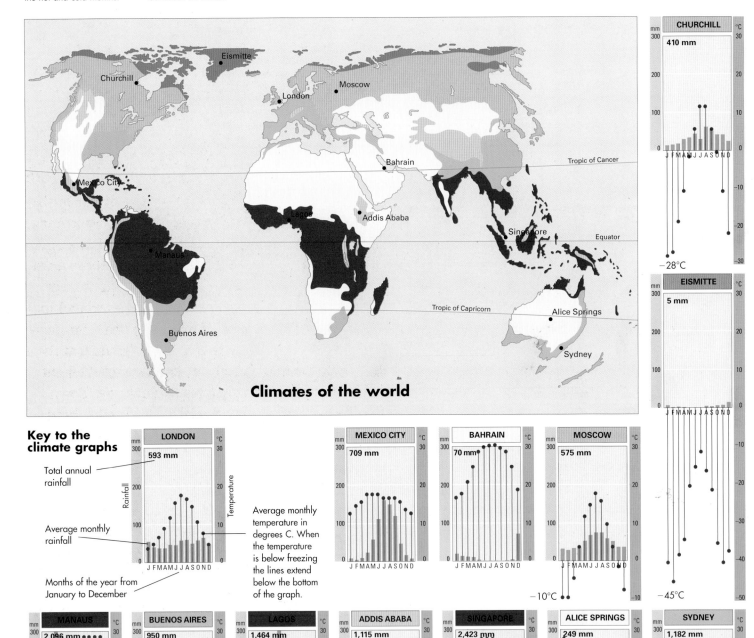

Climates of the world

Key to the climate graphs

Total annual rainfall

Average monthly rainfall

Months of the year from January to December

Average monthly temperature in degrees C. When the temperature is below freezing the lines extend below the bottom of the graph.

LONDON — 593 mm

CHURCHILL — 410 mm — −28°C

EISMITTE — 5 mm — −45°C

MEXICO CITY — 709 mm

BAHRAIN — 70 mm

MOSCOW — 575 mm — −10°C

MANAUS — 2,096 mm

BUENOS AIRES — 950 mm

LAGOS — 1,464 mm

ADDIS ABABA — 1,115 mm

SINGAPORE — 2,423 mm

ALICE SPRINGS — 249 mm

SYDNEY — 1,182 mm

Annual rainfall

Human, plant and animal life cannot live without water. The map on the right shows how much rain falls in different parts of the world. You can see that there is a lot of rain in some places near the Equator. In other places, like the desert areas of the world, there is very little rain. Few plants or animals can survive there. There is also very little rain in the cold lands of the north.

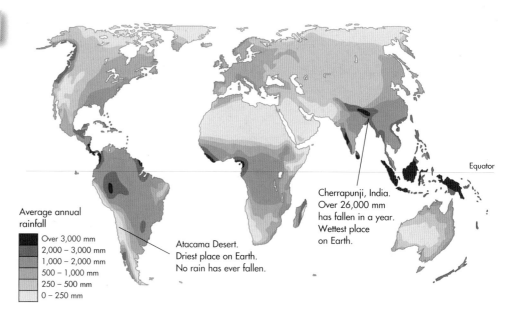

Average annual rainfall

- Over 3,000 mm
- 2,000 – 3,000 mm
- 1,000 – 2,000 mm
- 500 – 1,000 mm
- 250 – 500 mm
- 0 – 250 mm

Equator

Cherrapunji, India. Over 26,000 mm has fallen in a year. Wettest place on Earth.

Atacama Desert. Driest place on Earth. No rain has ever fallen.

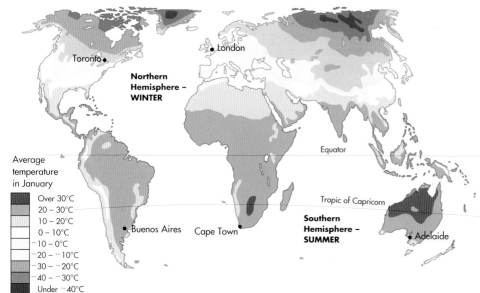

Average temperature in January

- Over 30°C
- 20 – 30°C
- 10 – 20°C
- 0 – 10°C
- −10 – 0°C
- −20 – −10°C
- −30 – −20°C
- −40 – −30°C
- Under −40°C

Toronto

London

Northern Hemisphere – WINTER

Equator

Tropic of Capricorn

Buenos Aires   Cape Town

Southern Hemisphere – SUMMER

Adelaide

January temperature

In December, it is winter in the northern hemisphere. It is hot in the southern continents and cold in the northern continents. The North Pole is tilted away from the sun. It is overhead in the regions around the Tropic of Capricorn. This means that there are about 14 hours of daylight in Buenos Aires, Cape Town and Adelaide, and only about 8 hours in London and Toronto.

July temperature

In July, it is summer in the northern hemisphere and winter in the southern hemisphere. It is warmer in the northern lands and colder in the south. The North Pole is tilted towards the sun. This means that in London and Toronto there are about 16 hours of daylight, but in Buenos Aires, Cape Town and Adelaide there are just under 10 hours.

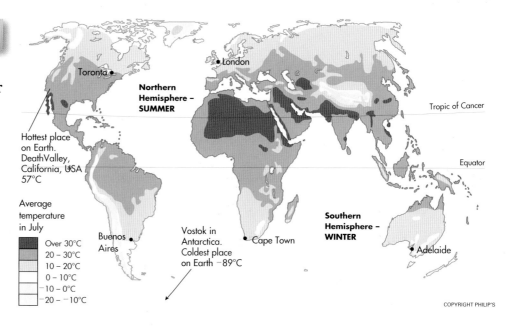

Toronto

London

Northern Hemisphere – SUMMER

Tropic of Cancer

Hottest place on Earth. Death Valley, California, USA 57°C

Equator

Average temperature in July

- Over 30°C
- 20 – 30°C
- 10 – 20°C
- 0 – 10°C
- −10 – 0°C
- −20 – −10°C

Buenos Aires

Vostok in Antarctica. Coldest place on Earth −89°C

Cape Town

Southern Hemisphere – WINTER

Adelaide

33

Climate change

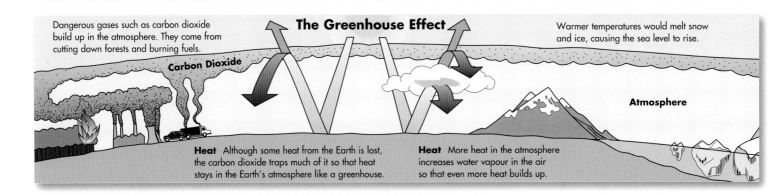

The Greenhouse Effect

Dangerous gases such as carbon dioxide build up in the atmosphere. They come from cutting down forests and burning fuels.

Carbon Dioxide

Warmer temperatures would melt snow and ice, causing the sea level to rise.

Atmosphere

Heat Although some heat from the Earth is lost, the carbon dioxide traps much of it so that heat stays in the Earth's atmosphere like a greenhouse.

Heat More heat in the atmosphere increases water vapour in the air so that even more heat builds up.

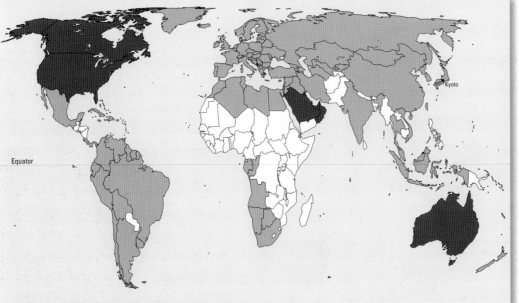

Equator

Carbon dioxide

- Major producers of carbon dioxide
- Other producers of carbon dioxide
- Countries producing very little carbon dioxide

This map shows which countries produce the most carbon dioxide per person. The countries that contribute the most to global warming tend to be rich countries like the USA and Australia. Can you think of reasons why?

Global warming

Experts have studied climate data from all around the world. They agreed several years ago that climate change really was happening. Leaders of all the major countries in the world come together regularly to try and agree on what to do about it. This graph shows how temperatures might not rise as much if countries can cut their carbon dioxide emissions.

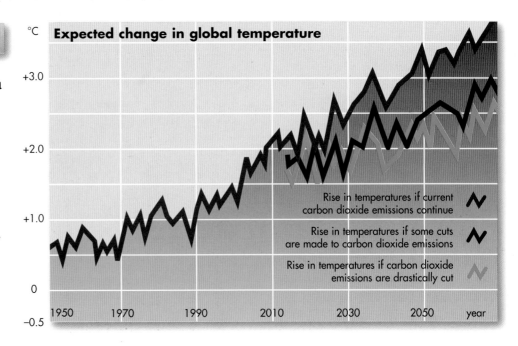

°C **Expected change in global temperature**

+3.0

+2.0

+1.0

0

−0.5

1950   1970   1990   2010   2030   2050   year

Rise in temperatures if current carbon dioxide emissions continue

Rise in temperatures if some cuts are made to carbon dioxide emissions

Rise in temperatures if carbon dioxide emissions are drastically cut

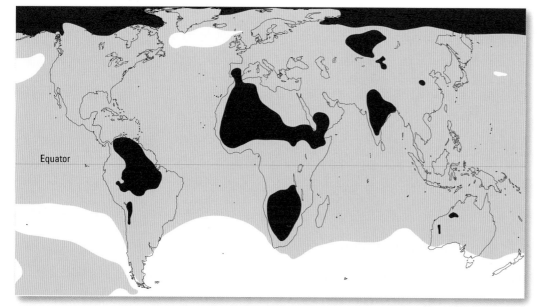

Temperature change

The expected change in temperature in the next 100 years

- ■ More than 5°C warmer
- ▨ Between 2°C and 5°C warmer
- □ Less than 2°C warmer

Compare this map with the map on the opposite page. The countries most affected by temperature change may not be the countries that are causing it.

Rainfall change

The expected change in the amount of rainfall in the next 100 years

- ▨ More rainfall
- ▨ Very little change in the amount of rainfall
- □ Less rainfall

As the global climate changes, some parts of the world will get more rainfall, while other parts will become drier. Can you think of the effects this might have?

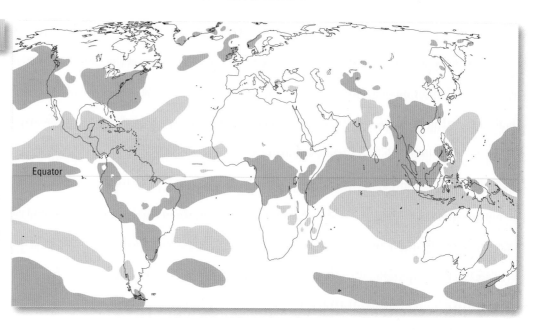

Sea level rise

- Areas at risk from rising sea level
- Areas with many low-lying islands

Warmer temperatures will result in ice caps melting in Antarctica and Greenland. Sea levels will rise and threaten low-lying coastal areas and islands. Many of the world's largest cities are threatened.

Forests, grasslands and wastes

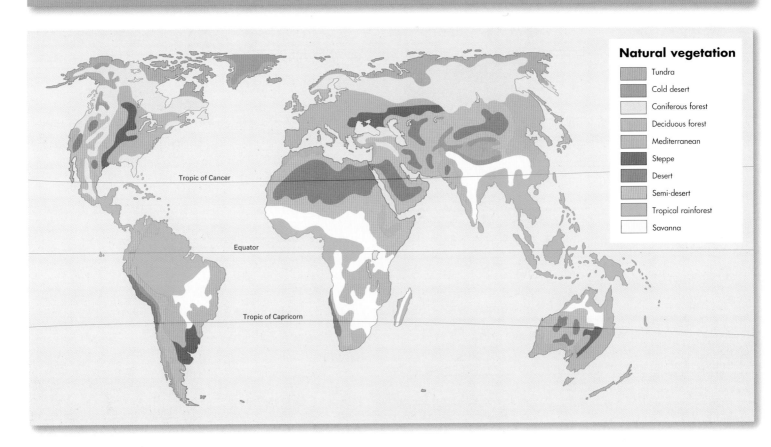

Natural vegetation

- Tundra
- Cold desert
- Coniferous forest
- Deciduous forest
- Mediterranean
- Steppe
- Desert
- Semi-desert
- Tropical rainforest
- Savanna

Tropic of Cancer

Equator

Tropic of Capricorn

The map above shows types of vegetation. The diagram below shows the effect of altitude on types of vegetation.

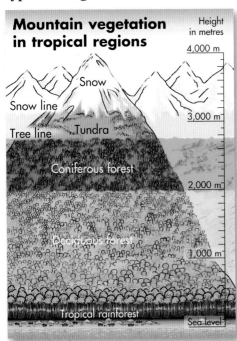

Mountain vegetation in tropical regions

Height in metres

4,000 m

Snow

Snow line

Tree line   Tundra

Coniferous forest

3,000 m

Deciduous forest

2,000 m

1,000 m

Tropical rainforest

Sea level

Tundra

Long, dry, cold winters. Grasses, moss, bog and dwarf trees.

Coniferous forest

Harsh winters, mild summers. Trees have leaves all year.

Mediterranean

Hot, dry summers. Mild wet winters. Plants adapt to the heat.

Desert

Rain is rare. Plants only grow at oases with underground water.

Tropical rainforest (jungle)

Very hot and wet all the year. Tall trees and lush vegetation.

Cold desert

Very cold with little rain or snow. No plants can grow.

Deciduous forest

Rain all year, cool winters. Trees shed leaves in winter.

Steppe

Some rain with a dry season. Grasslands with some trees.

Semi-desert

Poor rains, sparse vegetation. Grass with a few small trees.

Savanna

Mainly dry, but lush grass grows when the rains come.

Tundra

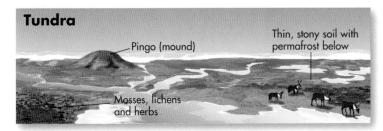

Pingo (mound)

Thin, stony soil with permafrost below

Mosses, lichens and herbs

Cold desert

No plants can grow

Coniferous forest

Evergreen conifers (spruces and firs)

Young tree saplings and small shrubs

Carpet of pine needles

Ferns and brambles on edge of forest

Yearly cycle of a deciduous forest

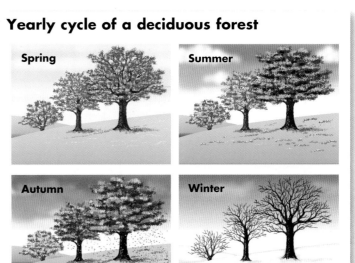

Spring

Summer

Autumn

Winter

Mediterranean

Small stunted trees

Scrub

Steppe

There are many plants in the steppe grasslands.

People planting crops can damage the natural habitat.

Tropical rainforest

Scattered trees with umbrella-shaped tops grow the highest.

Main layer of tall trees growing close together.

Creepers grow up the trees to reach the sunlight.

Ferns, mosses and small plants grow closest to the ground.

Desert

Sand blown into dunes by the wind

Palm trees

Cactus

Oasis

Semi-desert

Joshua trees

Grass and bush

Savanna

Dry season

Wet season

Volcanoes and earthquakes

The Earth's crust is made up of a series of pieces called plates. The cracks between them are called plate boundaries. They are shown on the map below. In some areas the plates move towards each other and the heavier plate is forced under the lighter plate. If the plates rub together, the Earth's surface can be shaken backwards and forwards. Where the shaking is very destructive this is called an earthquake. Tsunami waves are caused by underwater earthquakes (see map opposite). When plates are forced down to great depths, they can melt to form magma. Volcanoes erupt when this magma is forced upwards to the surface.

Major volcanic eruptions since 1900

Year	Volcano	Deaths
1902	Mount Pelee, Martinique	29,025
1902	Soufriere, St. Vincent	1,680
1902	Santa Maria, Guatemala	6,000
1911	Taal, Philippines	1.335
1919	Kelud, Indonesia	5,110
1951	Mount Lamington, Papua New Guinea	2,942
1963	Agung, Indonesia	1,184
1982	El Chichon, Mexico	2,000
1985	Nevado del Ruiz, Colombia	25,000
1986	Lake Nyos, Cameroon	1,700
1991	Pinatubo, Philippines	800

Volcanic regions

△ Volcanoes (active since 1700)

1991 Year of major volcanic eruptions since 1900

Plate boundaries

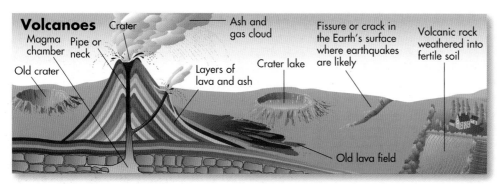

Volcanoes Crater — Ash and gas cloud

Magma chamber — Pipe or neck — Fissure or crack in the Earth's surface where earthquakes are likely — Volcanic rock weathered into fertile soil

Old crater — Crater lake — Layers of lava and ash

Old lava field

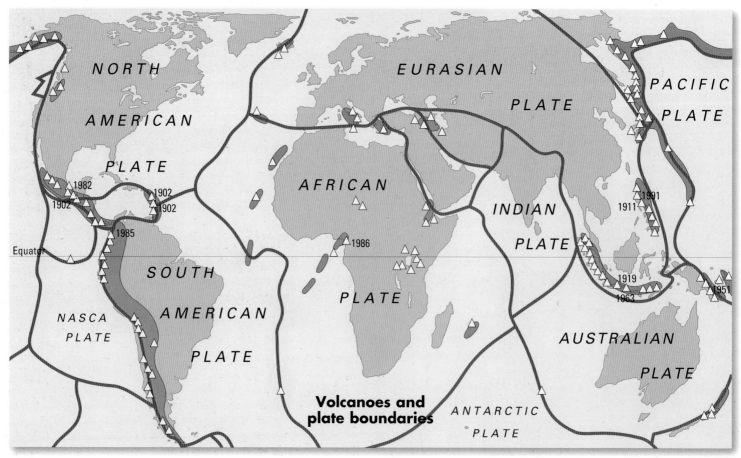

Volcanoes and plate boundaries

NORTH AMERICAN PLATE

EURASIAN PLATE

PACIFIC PLATE

AFRICAN PLATE

INDIAN PLATE

NASCA PLATE

SOUTH AMERICAN PLATE

AUSTRALIAN PLATE

ANTARCTIC PLATE

Equator

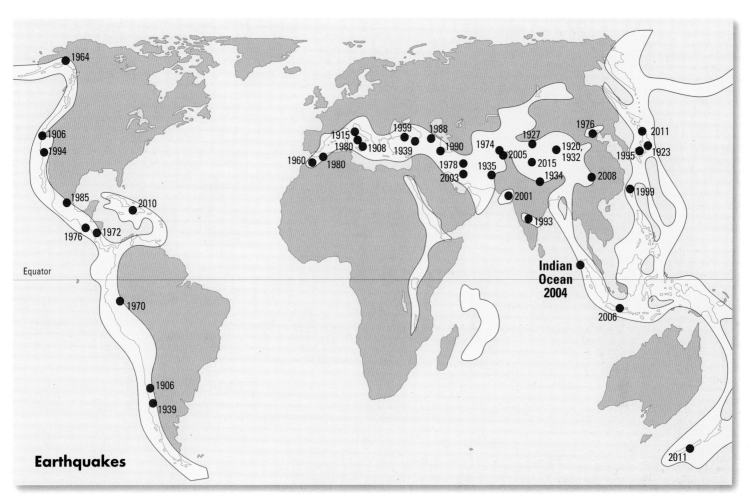

Earthquakes

Earthquake regions

● Major earthquakes since 1900 with dates

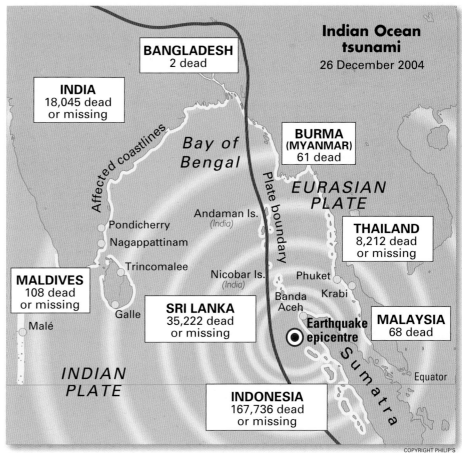

Indian Ocean tsunami
26 December 2004

BANGLADESH
2 dead

INDIA
18,045 dead or missing

BURMA (MYANMAR)
61 dead

Bay of Bengal

Affected coastlines

EURASIAN PLATE

Plate boundary

THAILAND
8,212 dead or missing

Andaman Is.
(India)

Pondicherry
Nagappattinam
Trincomalee

Nicobar Is.
(India)

Phuket
Krabi

Banda
Aceh

MALDIVES
108 dead or missing

SRI LANKA
35,222 dead or missing

Galle

Malé

Earthquake epicentre

MALAYSIA
68 dead

Sumatra

Equator

INDIAN PLATE

INDONESIA
167,736 dead or missing

COPYRIGHT PHILIP'S

Major earthquakes since 1900

Year	Location	Magnitude	Deaths
1908	Messina, Italy	7.5	83,000
1915	Avezzano, Italy	7.5	30,000
1920	Gansu, China	8.6	180,000
1923	Yokohama, Japan	8.3	143,000
1927	Nan Shan, China	8.3	200,000
1932	Gansu, China	7.6	70,000
1970	Northern Peru	7.8	66,794
1976	Tangshan, China	8.2	255,000
1988	Armenia	6.8	55,000
1993	Maharashtra, India	6.4	30,000
2001	Gujarat, India	7.7	14,000
2003	Bam, Iran	7.1	30,000
2004	Sumatra, Indonesia	9.0	230,000
2005	Northern Pakistan	7.6	74,000
2008	Sichuan, China	7.9	70,000
2010	Haiti	7.0	230,000
2011	Northern Japan	9.0	22,600
2015	Central Nepal	7.8	8,500

Farming and fishing

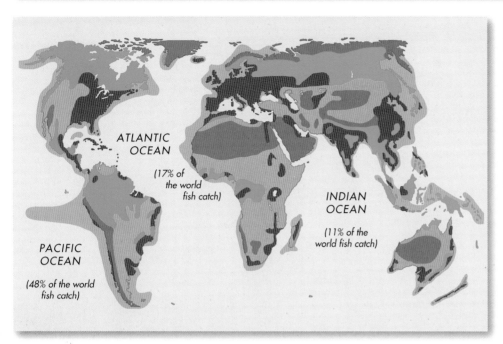

ATLANTIC OCEAN

(17% of the world fish catch)

INDIAN OCEAN

(11% of the world fish catch)

PACIFIC OCEAN

(48% of the world fish catch)

How the land is used

Forest areas with timber. Some hunting and fishing. Some farming in the tropics.

Deserts and wastelands

Animal farming on large farms (ranches)

Farming of crops and animals on large and small farms

Main fishing areas

Deserts and wastelands cover 32% of the world's total land area. Forests cover a further 30%. What percentage of the total land area does that leave for the farming of crops and animals?

The importance of agriculture

Over half the people work in agriculture

Between a quarter and half the people work in agriculture

Between one in ten and a quarter of the people work in agriculture

Less than one in ten of the people work in agriculture

A hundred years ago about 80% of the world's population worked in agriculture. Today it is only about 30% but agriculture is still very important in some countries.

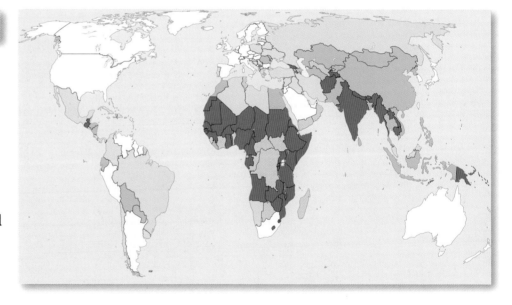

Methods of fishing

There are two types of sea fishing:

1. **Deep-sea fishing** using large trawlers which often stay at sea for many weeks.

2. **Inshore fishing** using small boats, traps and nets up to 70 km from the coast.

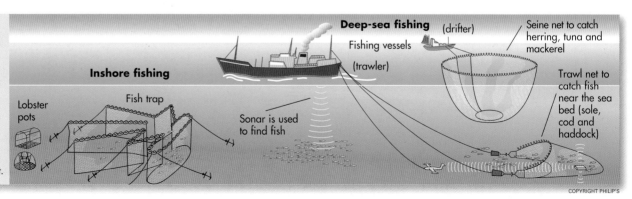

Inshore fishing

Lobster pots

Fish trap

Sonar is used to find fish

Deep-sea fishing (drifter)

Fishing vessels

(trawler)

Seine net to catch herring, tuna and mackerel

Trawl net to catch fish near the sea bed (sole, cod and haddock)

Energy resources

Oil and gas resources

![Oilfield symbol] Oilfields

![Natural gasfield symbol] Natural gasfields

![Arrow symbol] Main routes for transporting oil and gas by tanker

Crude oil is drilled from deep in the Earth's crust. The oil is then refined so that it can be used in different industries. Oil is used to make petrol and is also very important in the chemical industry. Natural gas is often found in the same places as oil.

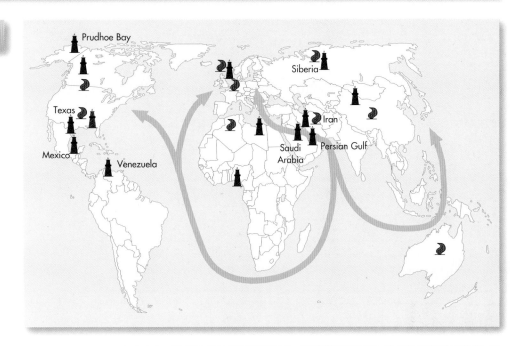

Coal resources

![Hard coal symbol] Hard coal (bituminous)

![Lignite symbol] Lignite (soft brown coal)

![Arrow symbol] Main routes for transporting coal

Coal is a fuel that comes from forests and swamps that rotted millions of years ago and have been crushed by layers of rock. The coal is cut out of the rock from deep mines and also from open-cast mines where the coal is nearer the surface. The oldest type of coal is hard. The coal formed more recently is softer.

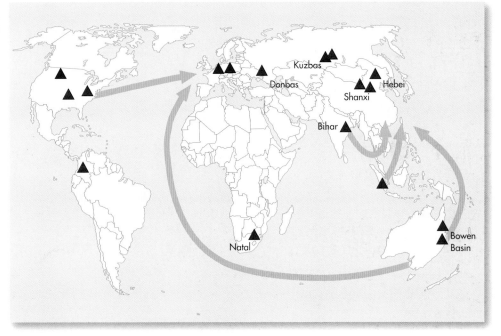

Renewable resources

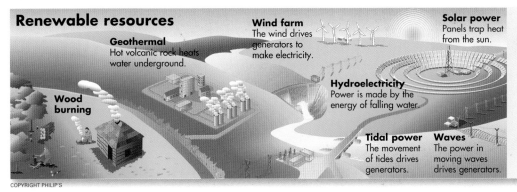

Geothermal
Hot volcanic rock heats water underground.

Wood burning

Wind farm
The wind drives generators to make electricity.

Solar power
Panels trap heat from the sun.

Hydroelectricity
Power is made by the energy of falling water.

Tidal power
The movement of tides drives generators.

Waves
The power in moving waves drives generators.

Oil, gas and coal are all resources which provide energy. Once these resources have been used up, they cannot be replaced. They are called **non-renewable resources**.

Energy is also provided by the sun, wind, waves, tides, and hot water from deep in the Earth. These resources will never run out. They are called **renewable resources**.

Transport and tourism

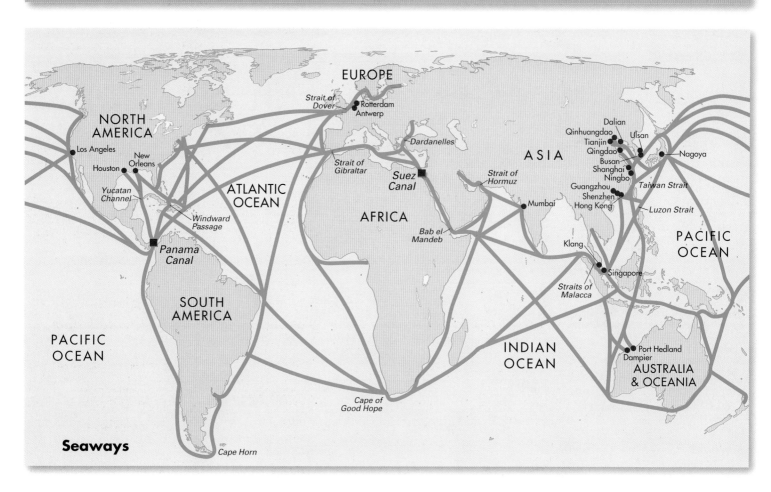

Seaways

— Main shipping routes

• The biggest seaports in the world

Sea transport is used for goods that are too bulky or heavy to go by air or land. The main shipping routes are between North America, Europe and the Far East.

Panama Canal and Suez Canal

These two important canals cut through narrow pieces of land. Can you work out how much shorter the journeys are by using the canals?

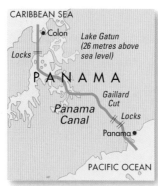

Panama Canal

• Opened in 1914
• 82 km long
• 13,000 ships a year
• Average toll $54,000
• Locks are needed in the Panama Canal to go between the Caribbean Sea and the Pacific Ocean

Suez Canal

• Opened in 1870
• 162 km long
• 21,000 ships a year
• Average toll $250,000
• The Suez Canal has no locks between the Mediterranean Sea and the Red Sea

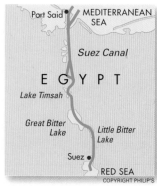

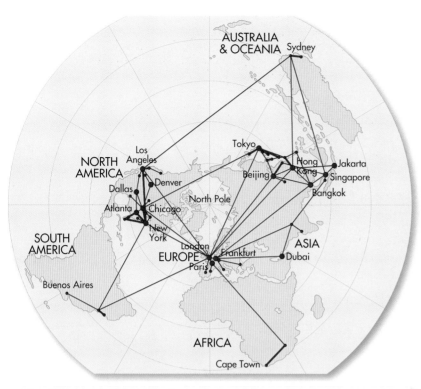

Airways

This map has the North Pole at its centre. It shows how much air traffic connects Europe, North America and Eastern Asia. You can see the long distances in the USA and Asia that are covered by air.

- ● Large international airports (over 50 million passengers a year)
- · Other important airports
- ━━ Heavily used air routes
- ── Other important air routes

Tourism

In 2013 there were 1,087 billion tourists visiting foreign countries. The most popular country to visit was France, followed by the USA, Spain and China.

- ☐ Ski resorts
- ▨ Centres of entertainment
- ■ Cultural and historical centres
- ▨ Places of pilgrimage
- ▨ Places of great natural beauty
- ☐ Coastal resorts

Air distances (kilometres)

	Buenos Aires	Cape Town	London	Los Angeles	New York	Sydney	Tokyo
Buenos Aires		6,880	11,128	9,854	8,526	11,760	18,338
Cape Town	6,880		9,672	16,067	12,551	10,982	14,710
London	11,128	9,672		8,752	5,535	17,005	9,584
Los Angeles	9,854	16,067	8,752		3,968	12,052	8,806
New York	8,526	12,551	5,535	3,968		16,001	10,869
Sydney	11,760	10,982	17,005	12,052	16,001		7,809
Tokyo	18,338	14,710	9,584	8,806	10,869	7,809	

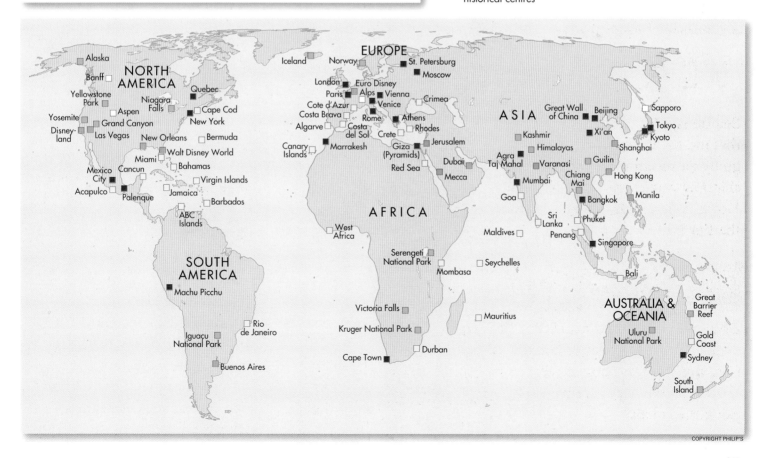

Rich and poor

All countries have both rich and poor people but some countries have more poor people than others. The amount of food that people have to eat and the age that they die can often depend on where they live in the world. The world can be divided into two parts – the rich and the poor.

The rich countries are mostly in the North and the poor countries are mostly in the South. The map below shows which countries are rich and which are poor. The list on the right shows some contrasts between rich and poor. Some of these contrasts can be seen in the maps on these pages.

Rich	**Poor**
• Good health	• Poor health
• Well educated	• Poorly educated
• Well fed	• Poorly fed
• Small families	• Large families
• Many industries	• Few industries
• Few farmers	• Many farmers
• Give aid	• Receive aid

Poor countries have over three-quarters of the world's population but less than a quarter of its wealth.

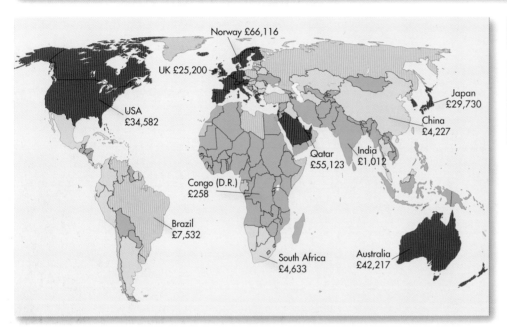

Income

■	Very rich countries
■	Rich countries
■	Poor countries
■	Very poor countries

The map shows how much money there is to spend on each person in a country. This is called income per person – this is worked out by dividing the wealth of a country by its population. The map gives examples of rich and poor countries.

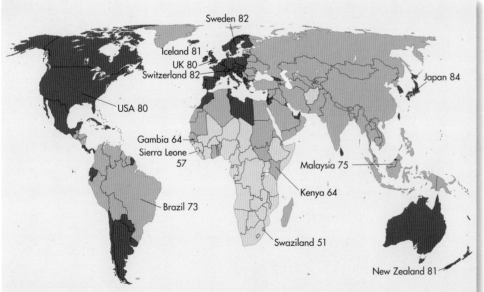

How long do people live?

This is the average age when people die

■	Over 75 years
■	60 – 75 years
■	Under 60 years

The average age of death is called life expectancy. In the world as a whole, the average life expectancy is 68 years. Some of the highest and lowest ages of death are shown on the map.

Food and famine

Below the amount of food they need

Above the amount of food they need

Over a third above the amount of food they need

 ★ Major famines since 1980

If people do not have enough to eat they become unhealthy. This map shows where in the world people have less than and more than the amount of food they need to live a healthy life.

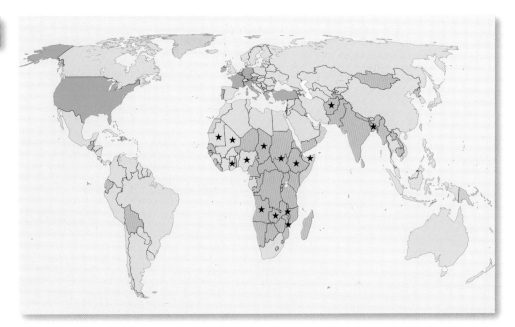

Reading and writing

Over half the adults cannot read or write

Between a quarter and a half of the adults cannot read or write

Less than a quarter of the adults cannot read or write

The map shows the proportion of adults in each country who cannot read or write a simple sentence. Can you think of some reasons why more people cannot read or write in some places in the world than in others?

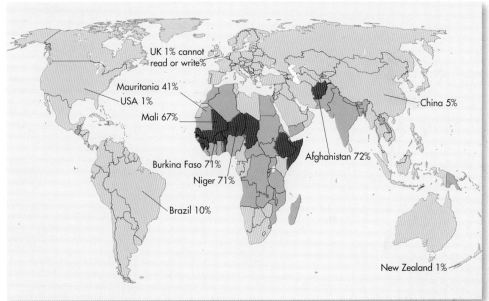

UK 1% cannot read or write%

Mauritania 41%

USA 1%

Mali 67%

China 5%

Afghanistan 72%

Burkina Faso 71%

Niger 71%

Brazil 10%

New Zealand 1%

Development aid

Over £25 received per person each year

Up to £25 received per person each year

Up to £100 given per person each year

Over £100 given per person each year

Countries that receive or give no aid

Some countries receive aid from other countries. Money is one type of aid. It is used to help with food, health and education problems. The map shows how much different countries give or receive.

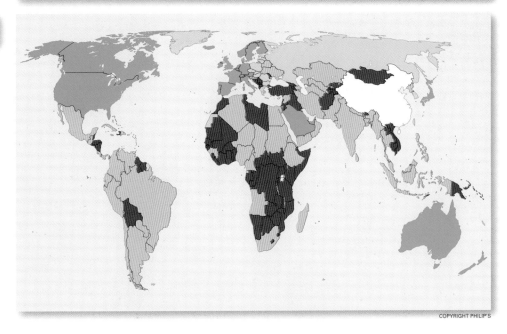

COPYRIGHT PHILIP'S

45

Peoples and cities

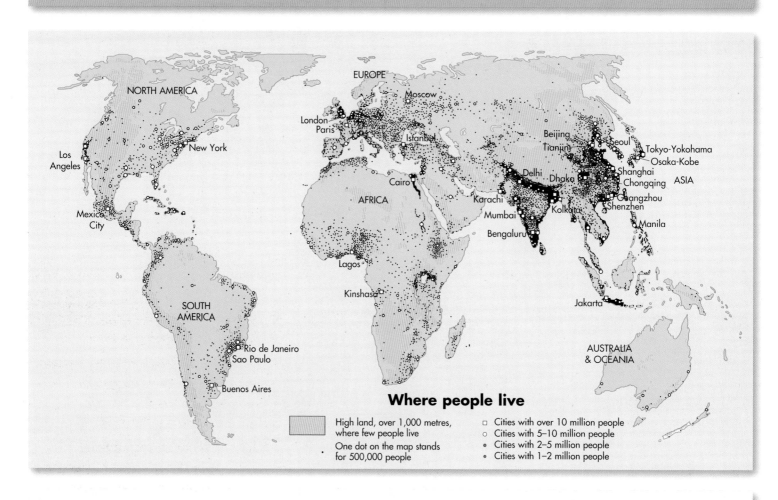

Where people live

▨	High land, over 1,000 metres, where few people live
·	One dot on the map stands for 500,000 people

□	Cities with over 10 million people
○	Cities with 5–10 million people
◦	Cities with 2–5 million people
·	Cities with 1–2 million people

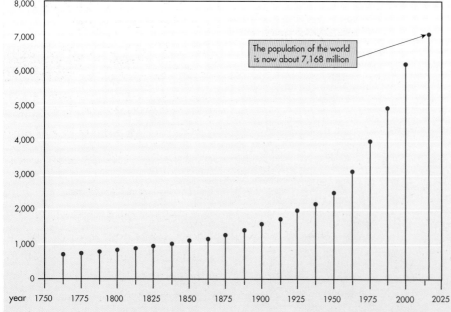

The growth of the population of the world 1750–2014

million people

The population of the world is now about 7,168 million

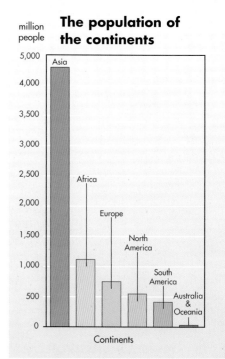

The population of the continents

million people

Continents

Largest nations

(population of countries in millions)

1. China 1,356
2. India 1,236
3. USA 319
4. Indonesia 254
5. Brazil 203
6. Pakistan 196
7. Nigeria 177
8. Bangladesh 166
9. Russia 142
10. Japan 127
11. Mexico 120
12. Philippines 108
13. Ethiopia 97
14. Vietnam 93
15. Egypt 87
16. Turkey 82
17. Germany 81
18. Iran 81
19. Congo (Dem. Rep.) 77
20. Thailand 68
21. France 66
22. UK 64

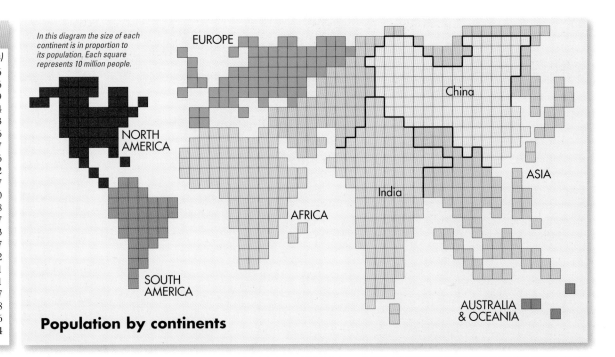

In this diagram the size of each continent is in proportion to its population. Each square represents 10 million people.

Population by continents

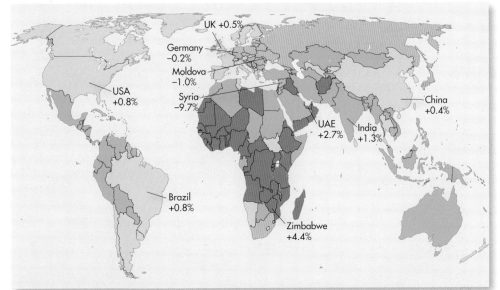

Increase and decrease

Annual rate of change in 2014

	Over 2% gain in the number of people
	Between 1% and 2% gain
	Under 1% gain
	Loss in the number of people

The map shows the rate of change in the number of people in each country. The largest increases are in poor countries in Africa and Asia. The number of people living in some richer countries is decreasing.

Living in cities

Urban population as a percentage of the total population in 2013

	Over three-quarters of the population live in cities
	Between a half and three-quarters live in cities
	Less than half live in cities

In 2008, for the first time in history, more than half of the world's population lived in cities. Why do you think people move from farms and villages to towns and cities?

47

Countries of the world

North America

(see pages 58–59)

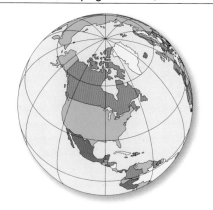

South America

(see pages 60–61)

Africa

(see pages 54–55)

These pages show different maps of the world. The large map shows the world cut through the Pacific Ocean and opened out on to flat paper. The smaller maps of the continents are views of the globe looking down on each of the continents.

Larger maps of the continents appear on the following pages. They show more cities than on this map.

■ Cities with more than 10 million people

48

Europe

(see pages 50–51)

Asia

(see pages 52–53)

Oceania

(see pages 56–57)

ALB.	= Albania	LUX.	= Luxembourg
ARM.	= Armenia	MAC.	= Macedonia
AZER.	= Azerbaijan	M.	= Montenegro
BELG.	= Belgium	NETH.	= Netherlands
B.-H.	= Bosnia-Herzegovina	S.	= Serbia
CR.	= Croatia	SLO.	= Slovenia
CZECH.	= Czech Republic	SWITZ.	= Switzerland
DOM. REP.	= Dominican Republic	U.A.E.	= United Arab Emirates
K.	= Kosovo	U.K.	= United Kingdom
LEB.	= Lebanon	U.S.A.	= United States of America

COPYRIGHT PHILIP'S

Europe

Largest countries – by area

(thousand square kilometres)

1. Russia....................... 17,075
2. Ukraine 604
3. France 552
4. Spain 498

Largest countries – by population

(million people)

1. Russia. 142
2. Germany 81
3. France 66
4. United Kingdom 64

Largest cities

(million people)

1. Istanbul (TURKEY) 14.2
2. Moscow (RUSSIA) 12.2
3. Paris (FRANCE) 10.8
4. London (UK) 10.3

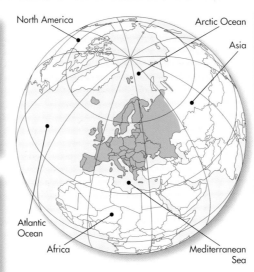

- *Europe is the second smallest continent. It is one-fifth the size of Asia. Australia is slightly smaller than Europe.*
- *The Ural Mountains form the eastern boundary of Europe.*
- *Great Britain is the largest island in Europe.*

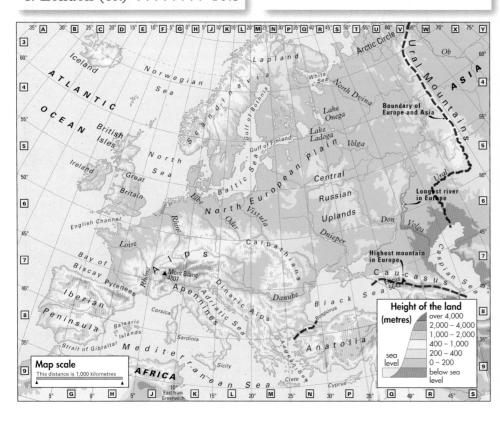

Height of the land
(metres)

- over 4,000
- 2,000 – 4,000
- 1,000 – 2,000
- 400 – 1,000
- 200 – 400
- 0 – 200
- below sea level

Map scale
This distance is 1,000 kilometres

Asia

Largest countries – by area
(thousand square kilometres)

1. Russia 17,075
2. China 9,597
3. India 3,287

Largest countries – by population
(million people)

1. China 1,356
2. India 1,236
3. Indonesia 254
4. Pakistan 196

Largest cities
(million people)

1. Tokyo (JAPAN) 38.0
2. Delhi (INDIA) 25.7
3. Shanghai (CHINA) 23.7
4. Mumbai (INDIA) 21.0
5. Beijing (CHINA) 20.4

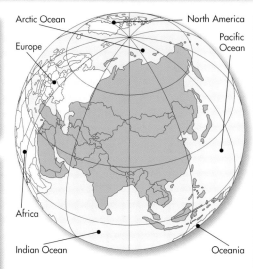

- Asia is the largest continent. It is twice the size of North America.

- It is a continent of long rivers. Many of Asia's rivers are longer than Europe's longest river.

- Asia contains well over half of the world's population.

Map information

■●● Cities ——— Country boundary

★ Capital city ▢ Sea and lakes

Ⓐ Index square - see index

Map scale
This distance is 2,000 kilometres

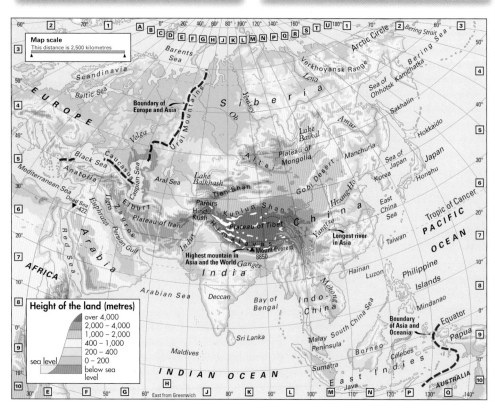

Map scale
This distance is 2,500 kilometres

Height of the land (metres)
over 4,000
2,000 – 4,000
1,000 – 2,000
400 – 1,000
200 – 400
0 – 200
sea level
below sea level

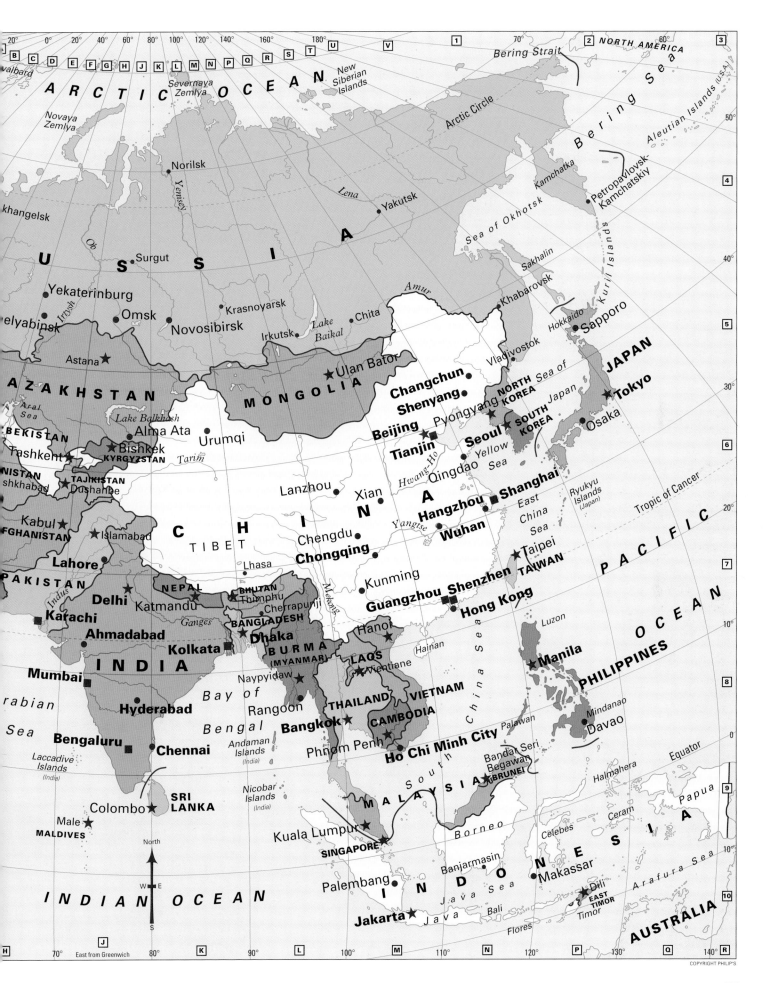

ARCTIC OCEAN

Bering Strait

NORTH AMERICA

Bering Sea

Aleutian Islands (U.S.A.)

Arctic Circle

Novaya Zemlya

Severnaya Zemlya

New Siberian Islands

...khangelsk

Norilsk

Yenisey

Lena

Yakutsk

Kamchatka

Petropavlovsk-Kamchatskiy

R U S S I A

Surgut

Yekaterinburg

Ob

Irtysh

...elyabinsk

Omsk

Novosibirsk

Krasnoyarsk

Irkutsk

Lake Baikal

Chita

Amur

Khabarovsk

Sea of Okhotsk

Sakhalin

Kuril Islands

Hokkaido

Sapporo

JAPAN

Astana

KAZAKHSTAN

Aral Sea

Lake Balkhash

MONGOLIA

Ulan Bator

Changchun

Shenyang

Vladivostok

Sea of Japan

Tokyo

...BEKISTAN

Tashkent

Alma Ata

Urumqi

Beijing

Pyongyang

NORTH KOREA

SOUTH KOREA

Osaka

Bishkek

KYRGYZSTAN

Tarim

Tianjin

Seoul

Yellow

...NISTAN

TAJIKISTAN

...shkabad

Dushanbe

Lanzhou

Xian

C H I N A

Qingdao

Hwang-Ho

Sea

Shanghai

East China Sea

Ryukyu Islands (Japan)

Tropic of Cancer

Kabul

Islamabad

C

TIBET

Chengdu

Chongqing

Yangtse

Hangzhou

Wuhan

AFGHANISTAN

Lahore

Lhasa

Kunming

Taipei

TAIWAN

PACIFIC

PAKISTAN

Indus

NEPAL

Katmandu

BHUTAN

Thimphu

Mekong

Guangzhou

Shenzhen

Delhi

Ganges

Cherrapunji

BANGLADESH

Hong Kong

Karachi

Ahmadabad

Kolkata

Dhaka

BURMA (MYANMAR)

Hanoi

Luzon

OCEAN

Mumbai

I N D I A

Naypyidaw

LAOS

Vientiane

Hainan

Manila

PHILIPPINES

...rabian Sea

Hyderabad

Rangoon

THAILAND

VIETNAM

Mindanao

Davao

Bengaluru

Chennai

Bay of Bengal

Bangkok

CAMBODIA

Phnom Penh

Ho Chi Minh City

Palawan

South China Sea

Andaman Islands (India)

Laccadive Islands (India)

Colombo

SRI LANKA

Nicobar Islands (India)

MALAYSIA

Bandar Seri Begawan

BRUNEI

Halmahera

Equator

Papua

Male

MALDIVES

North

Kuala Lumpur

SINGAPORE

Borneo

Celebes

Ceram

INDIAN OCEAN

W E

S

Banjarmasin

I N D O N E S I A

Makassar

Arafura Sea

Palembang

Java Sea

Dili

EAST TIMOR

Jakarta

Java

Bali

Timor

Flores

AUSTRALIA

COPYRIGHT PHILIP'S

53

Africa

- Africa is the second largest continent. Asia is the largest.

- There are over 50 countries, some of them small in area and population. The population of Africa is growing more quickly than any other continent.

- Parts of Africa have a dry, desert climate. Other parts are tropical.

- The highest mountains run from north to south on the eastern side of Africa. The Great Rift Valley is a volcanic valley that was formed 10 to 20 million years ago by a crack in the Earth's crust. Mount Kenya and Kilimanjaro are examples of old volcanoes in the area.

- The Sahara is the largest desert in the world.

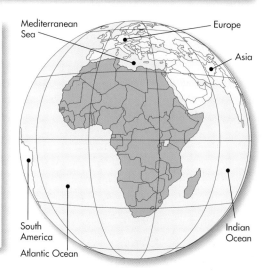

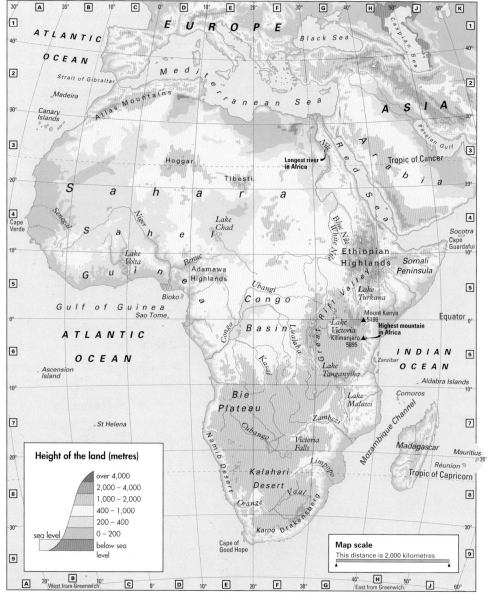

Largest countries – by area

(thousand square kilometres)

1. Algeria 2,382
2. Congo (Dem. Rep.) . . 2,345
3. Sudan. 1,886
4. Libya 1,760
5. Chad 1,284
6. Niger 1,267

Largest countries – by population

(million people)

1. Nigeria 177
2. Ethiopia 97
3. Egypt 87
4. Congo (Dem. Rep.) 77
5. Tanzania 50
6. South Africa. 48

Largest cities

(million people)

1. Cairo (EGYPT) 18.8
2. Lagos (NIGERIA) 13.1
3. Kinshasa (CONGO, D. R.) . 11.6
4. Johannesburg (S. AFRICA) . 9.4
5. Luanda (ANGOLA) 5.5

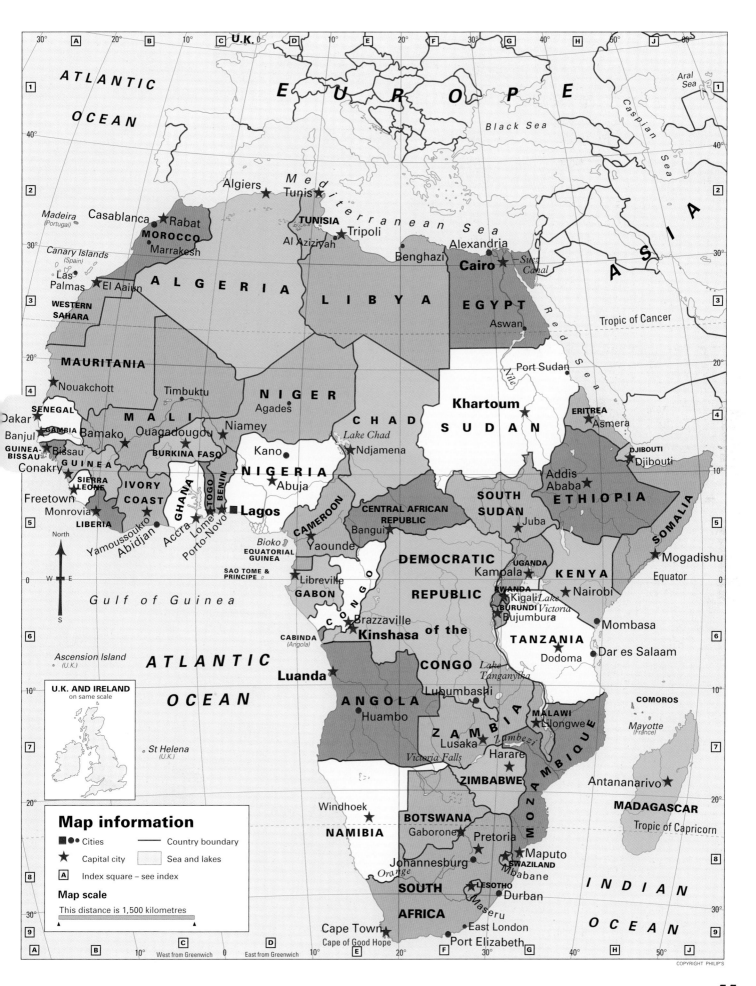

ATLANTIC OCEAN

E U R O P E

Aral Sea

Black Sea

Caspian Sea

A S I A

Madeira (Portugal)

Casablanca
Rabat
MOROCCO
Marrakesh

Algiers
Tunis
TUNISIA
Tripoli
Al Aziziyah

Mediterranean Sea

Benghazi
Alexandria
Cairo
Suez Canal

Canary Islands (Spain)
Las Palmas
El Aaiun
WESTERN SAHARA

A L G E R I A

L I B Y A

E G Y P T
Aswan
Red Sea

Tropic of Cancer

MAURITANIA
Nouakchott

Timbuktu
Agades

N I G E R

C H A D
Lake Chad
Ndjamena

Port Sudan

Khartoum
S U D A N

ERITREA
Asmera

DJIBOUTI
Djibouti

SENEGAL
Dakar
GAMBIA
Banjul
GUINEA-BISSAU
Bissau
Conakry
GUINEA
SIERRA LEONE
Freetown
Monrovia
LIBERIA

M A L I
Bamako
Ouagadougou
BURKINA FASO

Niamey

Kano

N I G E R I A
Abuja

Yamoussoukro
Abidjan
IVORY COAST
GHANA
Accra
TOGO
Lome
BENIN
Porto-Novo
Lagos

CAMEROON
Yaounde
Bioko
EQUATORIAL GUINEA
SAO TOME & PRINCIPE

CENTRAL AFRICAN REPUBLIC
Bangui

SOUTH SUDAN
Juba

Addis Ababa
E T H I O P I A

SOMALIA
Mogadishu

North

W   E
S

Gulf of Guinea

GABON
Libreville
CONGO

DEMOCRATIC

REPUBLIC

of the

CONGO

Brazzaville
Kinshasa
CABINDA (Angola)

UGANDA
Kampala
RWANDA
Kigali
BURUNDI
Bujumbura
Lake Victoria

K E N Y A
Nairobi

Equator

Mombasa

Ascension Island (U.K.)

ATLANTIC

OCEAN

Luanda

A N G O L A
Huambo

Lubumbashi
Lake Tanganyika

T A N Z A N I A
Dodoma
Dar es Salaam

St Helena (U.K.)

U.K. AND IRELAND
on same scale

COMOROS

Mayotte (France)

MALAWI
Lilongwe

Z A M B I A
Lusaka
Zambezi
Victoria Falls
Harare
ZIMBABWE

M O Z A M B I Q U E

MADAGASCAR
Antananarivo

Tropic of Capricorn

Windhoek

NAMIBIA

BOTSWANA
Gaborone

Pretoria
Johannesburg
Orange

SOUTH
AFRICA

LESOTHO
Maseru

Maputo
SWAZILAND
Mbabane

INDIAN

OCEAN

Durban
East London

Cape Town
Cape of Good Hope
Port Elizabeth

Map information

- ■ ● Cities
- ★ Capital city
- A Index square – see index
- —— Country boundary
- Sea and lakes

Map scale

This distance is 1,500 kilometres

30° 20° 10° U.K. 0 10° 20° 30° 40° 50° 60°

West from Greenwich   East from Greenwich

COPYRIGHT PHILIP'S

55

Australia and Oceania

- The continent is often called Oceania. It is made up of the huge island of Australia and thousands of smaller islands in the Pacific Ocean.

- It is the smallest continent, only about a sixth the size of Asia.

- The highest mountain is on the Indonesian part of New Guinea which many consider to be part of Asia.

Largest countries – by area
(thousand square kilometres)

1. Australia 7,741
2. Papua New Guinea . . . 463
3. New Zealand 271

Largest countries – by population
(million people)

1. Australia 23
2. Papua New Guinea 7

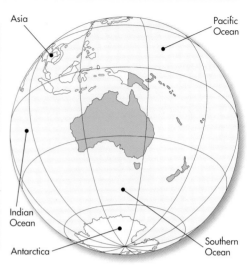

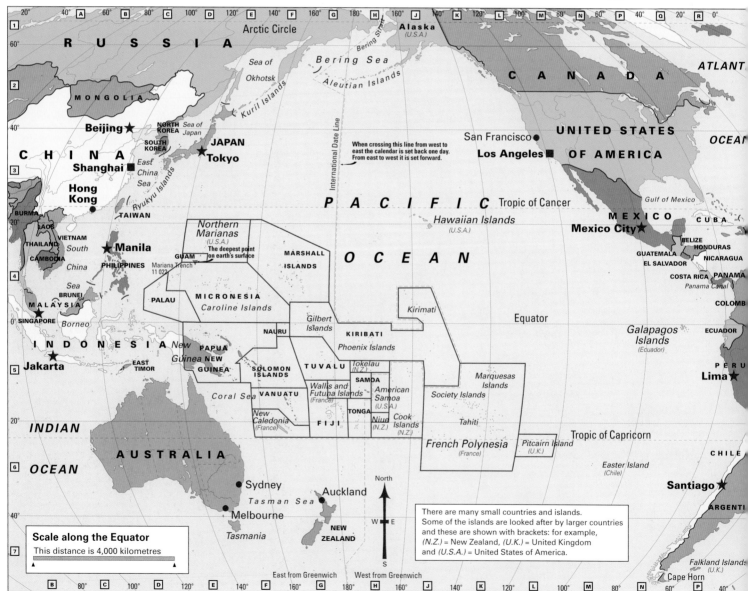

There are many small countries and islands. Some of the islands are looked after by larger countries and these are shown with brackets: for example, (N.Z.) = New Zealand, (U.K.) = United Kingdom and (U.S.A.) = United States of America.

Scale along the Equator
This distance is 4,000 kilometres

When crossing this line from west to east the calendar is set back one day. From east to west it is set forward.

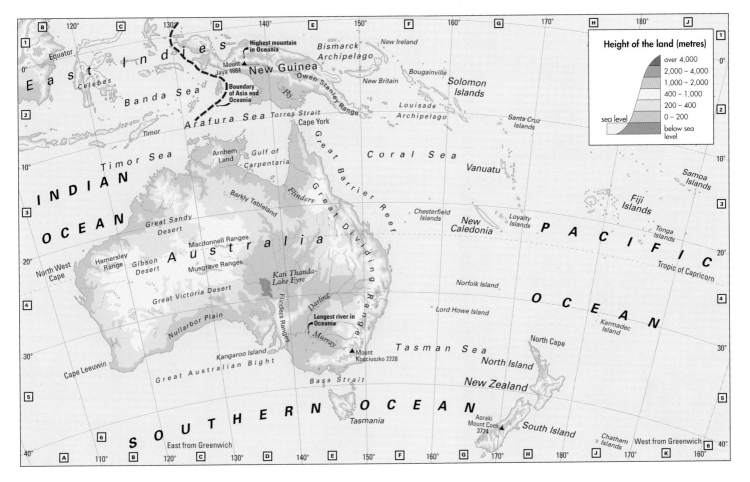

Height of the land (metres)

- over 4,000
- 2,000 – 4,000
- 1,000 – 2,000
- 400 – 1,000
- 200 – 400
- 0 – 200
- sea level
- below sea level

Top map labels:

East Indies

Equator

Celebes

Banda Sea

Timor

Bismarck Archipelago

New Ireland

New Guinea

Highest mountain in Oceania

Mount Jaya 4884

Boundary of Asia and Oceania

Owen Stanley Range

Fly

New Britain

Bougainville

Solomon Islands

Arafura Sea

Torres Strait

Cape York

Louisade Archipelago

INDIAN OCEAN

Timor Sea

Arnhem Land

Gulf of Carpentaria

Coral Sea

Vanuatu

Santa Cruz Islands

Samoa Islands

Barkly Tableland

Great Barrier Reef

Chesterfield Islands

New Caledonia

Loyalty Islands

Fiji Islands

Tonga Islands

North West Cape

Hamersley Range

Great Sandy Desert

Macdonnell Ranges

Australia

Great Dividing Range

Tropic of Capricorn

PACIFIC

Gibson Desert

Musgrave Ranges

Kati Thanda-Lake Eyre

Norfolk Island

Great Victoria Desert

Darling

Nullarbor Plain

Flinders Ranges

Longest river in Oceania

Murray

Lord Howe Island

Kermadec Island

OCEAN

Cape Leeuwin

Kangaroo Island

Mount Kosciuszko 2228

Tasman Sea

North Cape

North Island

Great Australian Bight

Bass Strait

New Zealand

SOUTHERN OCEAN

East from Greenwich

Tasmania

Aoraki Mount Cook 3724

South Island

Chatham Islands

West from Greenwich

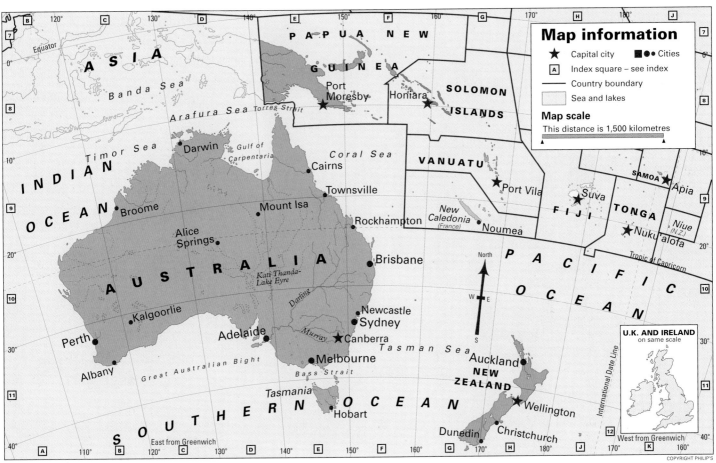

Map information

- ★ Capital city
- ■ ● ● Cities
- Ⓐ Index square – see index
- — Country boundary
- Sea and lakes

Map scale

This distance is 1,500 kilometres

Bottom map labels:

Equator

ASIA

Banda Sea

PAPUA NEW GUINEA

Port Moresby

Honiara

SOLOMON ISLANDS

Arafura Sea

Torres Strait

Darwin

Gulf of Carpentaria

Coral Sea

VANUATU

Port Vila

Broome

Cairns

Townsville

SAMOA

Apia

INDIAN OCEAN

Timor Sea

Mount Isa

Rockhampton

New Caledonia (France)

Noumea

Suva

FIJI

TONGA

Nuku'alofa

Niue (N.Z.)

Alice Springs

Brisbane

Tropic of Capricorn

AUSTRALIA

Kati Thanda-Lake Eyre

North

Kalgoorlie

Darling

Newcastle

Sydney

PACIFIC

Perth

Adelaide

Murray

Canberra

OCEAN

Albany

Melbourne

Great Australian Bight

Bass Strait

Tasman Sea

Auckland

NEW ZEALAND

Tasmania

Hobart

Wellington

SOUTHERN OCEAN

East from Greenwich

Dunedin

Christchurch

West from Greenwich

International Date Line

U.K. AND IRELAND on same scale

COPYRIGHT PHILIP'S

North America

- North America is the third largest continent. It is half the size of Asia. It stretches almost from the Equator to the North Pole.

- Three countries – Canada, the United States and Mexico – make up most of the continent.

- Greenland, the largest island in the world, is included within North America.

- In the east there are a series of large lakes. These are called the Great Lakes. A large waterfall called Niagara Falls is between Lake Erie and Lake Ontario. The St Lawrence River connects the Great Lakes with the Atlantic Ocean.

- North and South America are joined by a narrow strip of land called the Isthmus of Panama.

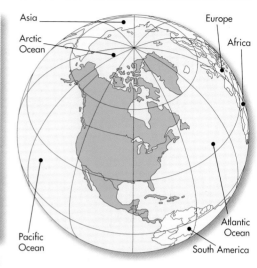

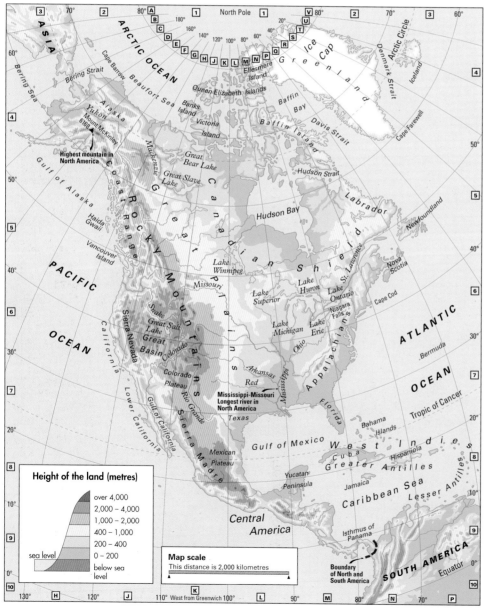

Largest countries – by area

(thousand square kilometres)

1. Canada	9,971
2. United States	9,629
3. Greenland	2,176
4. Mexico	1,958
5. Nicaragua	130
6. Honduras	112

Largest countries – by population

(million people)

1. United States	319
2. Mexico	120
3. Canada	35
4. Guatemala	15
5. Cuba	11
6. Dominican Republic	10

Largest cities

(million people)

1. Mexico City (MEXICO)	21.0
2. New York (USA)	20.0
3. Los Angeles (USA)	13.1
4. Chicago (USA)	9.5
5. Dallas (USA)	6.8

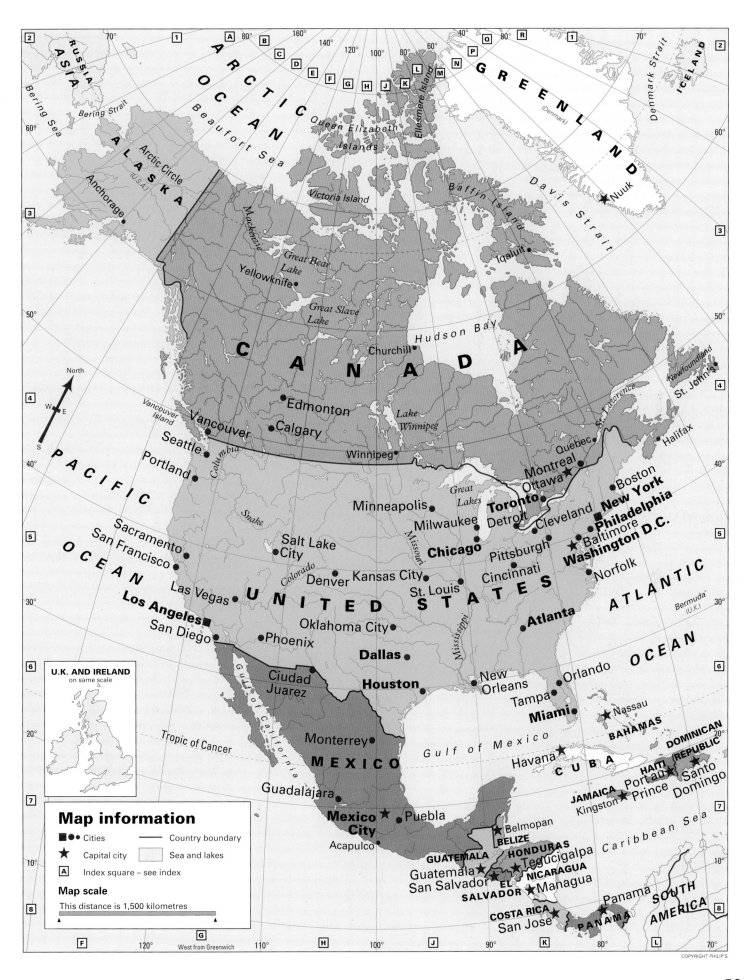

Map information

- ■●● Cities
- ⭐ Capital city
- Ⓐ Index square – see index
- ── Country boundary
- ▨ Sea and lakes

Map scale

This distance is 1,500 kilometres

U.K. AND IRELAND
on same scale

ASIA
RUSSIA
Bering Sea
Bering Strait

ARCTIC OCEAN
Beaufort Sea

ALASKA (USA)
Arctic Circle
Anchorage

Queen Elizabeth Islands
Victoria Island
Ellesmere Island

GREENLAND (Denmark)
Denmark Strait
ICELAND

Baffin Island
Davis Strait
Nuuk

Mackensie
Great Bear Lake
Yellowknife
Great Slave Lake
Iqaluit

CANADA
Churchill
Hudson Bay

St. Lawrence
Newfoundland
St. John's

Edmonton
Calgary
Lake Winnipeg
Quebec
Montreal
Halifax

Vancouver Island
Vancouver
Seattle
Columbia
Portland
Winnipeg
Ottawa
Boston

PACIFIC
OCEAN

Snake
Minneapolis
Milwaukee
Great Lakes
Toronto
Detroit
Cleveland
New York
Philadelphia
Baltimore
Washington D.C.

Sacramento
San Francisco
Salt Lake City
Chicago
Pittsburgh
Norfolk

Las Vegas
Denver
Colorado
Kansas City
Cincinnati
St. Louis

ATLANTIC
OCEAN
Bermuda (U.K.)

Los Angeles
San Diego
Phoenix
UNITED STATES
Oklahoma City
Missouri
Atlanta

Dallas
Houston
Mississippi
New Orleans
Orlando

Ciudad Juarez
Gulf of California
Tampa
Miami
Nassau
BAHAMAS

Tropic of Cancer
Monterrey
Gulf of Mexico
Havana
CUBA
DOMINICAN REPUBLIC
HAITI
Port au Prince
Santo Domingo

MEXICO
Guadalajara
JAMAICA
Kingston

Mexico City
Puebla
Belmopan
BELIZE
Caribbean Sea

Acapulco
GUATEMALA
Guatemala
San Salvador
HONDURAS
Tegucigalpa
NICARAGUA
Managua

EL SALVADOR
COSTA RICA
San Jose
Panama
PANAMA
SOUTH AMERICA

West from Greenwich

COPYRIGHT PHILIP'S

South America

- The Amazon is the second longest river in the world. The Nile is the longest river, but more water flows from the Amazon into the ocean than from any other river.

- The range of mountains called the Andes runs for over 7,500 km from north to south on the western side of the continent. There are many volcanoes in the Andes.

- Lake Titicaca is the largest lake in the continent. It has an area of 8,300 sq km and is 3,800 metres above sea level.

- Spanish and Portuguese are the principal languages spoken in South America.

- Brazil is the largest country in area and population, and has the largest city.

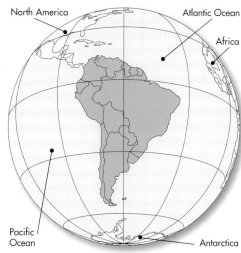

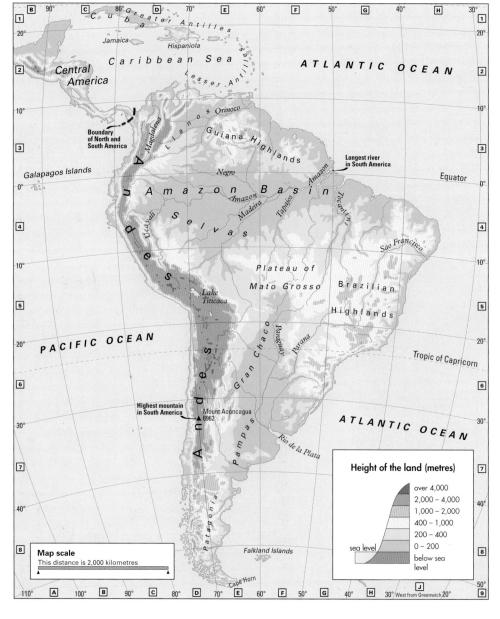

Largest countries – by area

(thousand square kilometres)

1. Brazil 8,514
2. Argentina 2,780
3. Peru 1,285
4. Colombia 1,139
5. Bolivia 1,099
6. Venezuela 912

Largest countries – by population

(million people)

1. Brazil 203
2. Colombia 46
3. Argentina 43
4. Peru 30
5. Venezuela 29
6. Chile 17

Largest cities

(million people)

1. Sao Paulo (BRAZIL) 21.1
2. Buenos Aires (ARGENTINA) 15.2
3. Rio de Janeiro (BRAZIL) . 12.9
4. Lima (PERU) 9.9
5. Bogota (COLOMBIA) 9.8

B 90° C 80° D 70° E 60° F 50° G 40° H

1 BAHAMAS **1**

20° **MEXICO** CUBA

DOMINICAN REPUBLIC PUERTO RICO (U.S.A.) VIRGIN ISLANDS (U.S.A.-U.K.)
ST KITTS & NEVIS
ANTIGUA & BARBUDA

BELIZE JAMAICA HAITI **ATLANTIC** **2**

2 GUATEMALA HONDURAS *Caribbean Sea* GUADELOUPE (France)
DOMINICA (France)
MARTINIQUE (France)
ST LUCIA
BARBADOS **OCEAN**

EL SALVADOR NICARAGUA

COSTA RICA CURACAO (Netherlands) ST VINCENT
GRENADA

Barranquilla *Panama Canal* Caracas Port of Spain
TRINIDAD & TOBAGO 10°

PANAMA Maracaibo Valencia **VENEZUELA** *Orinoco* Georgetown **3**

3 Medellin **Bogota** GUYANA Paramaribo Cayenne

COLOMBIA SURINAME **FRENCH GUIANA** (France)

Cali

Equator *Negro* *Amazon* Belem 0

Quito **ECUADOR** Sao Luis Fortaleza

Guayaquil Iquitos Manaus *Madeira* *Tapajos* Natal **4**

4 Chiclayo *Ucayali* **B R A Z I L** Joao Pessao

Trujillo Recife

PERU *Xingu* *Tocantins* *Sao Francisco* Maceio

Lima Cusco Salvador 10°

Arequipa *Lake Titicaca* La Paz Cuiaba Brasilia

5 **BOLIVIA** Goiania **5**

PACIFIC Sucre Belo Horizonte

Vitoria 20°

Antofagasta **PARAGUAY** *Parana* Campinas **Rio de Janeiro**

Tropic of Capricorn Asuncion **Sao Paulo** Curitiba

6 *OCEAN* Florianopolis **ATLANTIC** **6**

CHILE Tucuman Porto Alegre

North Cordoba URUGUAY 30°

Valparaiso Rosario **OCEAN**

Juan Fernandez (Chile) Santiago **Buenos Aires** Montevideo

7 Concepcion *Rio de la Plata* **7**

ARGENTINA 40°

Bahia Blanca

U.K. AND IRELAND
on same scale

8 **8**

Falkland Islands (U.K.)
Stanley

Punta Arenas *South Georgia (U.K.)* 50°

9 Cape Horn **9**
50° A 100° B 90° C 80° D 70° E 60° F 50° G 40° H 30° J 20°

Map information

■ ● ● Cities   —— Country boundary

★ Capital city   ▢ Sea and lakes

Ⓐ Index square – see index

Map scale

This distance is 1,500 kilometres

COPYRIGHT PHILIP'S

61

Polar Regions

The Polar Regions are the areas around the North Pole and the South Pole. The area around the North Pole is called the **Arctic** and the area around the South Pole is called the **Antarctic**. The sun never shines straight down on the Arctic or Antarctic so they are very cold – the coldest places on Earth. The Arctic consists of frozen water. Some parts of Northern Europe, North America and Asia are inside the Arctic Circle. A group of people called the Inuit live there.

Map information

- Cities and towns
★ Capital cities
- (Japan) Scientific stations in the Antarctic

Cross-section

Land covered in ice

Ice always in the sea

Ice sometimes in the sea

Map scale
This distance is 1,500 kilometres

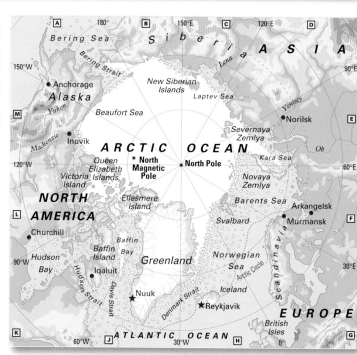

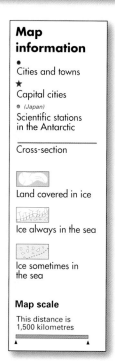

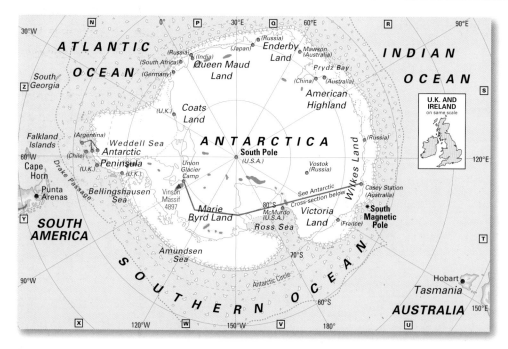

The Antarctic is a continent. It is bigger than Europe or Australia and has no permanent population. Most of the land consists of ice which is thousands of metres thick. At the edges, chunks of ice break off to make icebergs. These float out to sea. The diagram below shows a cross-section through Antarctica between two of the camps, Union Glacier Camp and Casey Station. It shows how thick the ice is on the ice sheets.

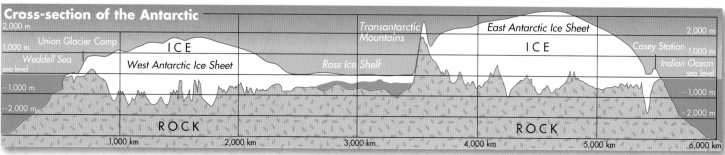

Cross-section of the Antarctic

Finding places

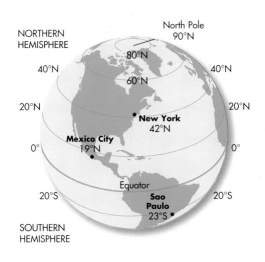

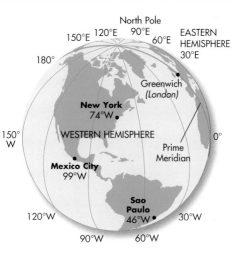

Latitude

These three maps show part of the Earth as if seen from thousands of kilometres above New York. Exactly halfway between the North and South Poles is an imaginary line called the Equator. It divides the Earth into north and south hemispheres and is numbered 0°. On either side of the Equator run parallel lines called lines of latitude.

Longitude

Maps have another set of lines running north to south linking the Poles. These lines are called lines of longitude. The line numbered 0° runs through Greenwich in London, England, and is called the Prime Meridian. The other lines of longitude are numbered up to 180° east and west of 0°. Longitude line 180° runs through the Pacific Ocean.

Map references

The latitude and longitude lines on maps form a grid. In this atlas, the grid lines are in blue, and on most maps are shown for every ten degrees. The numbers of the lines can be used to give a reference to show the location of a place on a map. The index in this atlas uses another way of finding places. It lists the rows of latitude as numbers and the columns of longitude as letters.

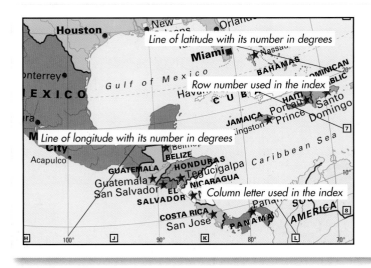

	Latitude	Longitude	Map page	Map letter-number
Lagos, Africa	6°N	3°E	55	D5
Mexico City, North America	19°N	99°W	59	H7
Moscow, Europe	55°N	37°E	51	Q4
Sao Paulo, South America	23°S	46°W	61	G6
Sydney, Oceania	34°S	151°E	57	F11
Tokyo, Asia	35°N	139°E	53	R5

This table shows the largest city in each continent with its latitude and longitude. Look for them on the maps in this atlas using the letter-number references.

Index of place names